| Oxford Shakespeare Topics

Staging in Shakespeare's Theatres

OXFORD SHAKESPEARE TOPICS

Published and Forthcoming Titles Include:

Oxford Shakespeare Topics

GENERAL EDITORS: PETER HOLLAND AND STANLEY WELLS

Staging in Shakespeare's Theatres

ANDREW GURR

AND

MARIKO ICHIKAWA

OXFORD
UNIVERSITY PRESS

OXFORD

UNIVERSITY PRESS

Great Clarendon Street, Oxford OX2 6DP

Oxford University Press is a department of the University of Oxford.
It furthers the University's objective of excellence in research, scholarship,
and education by publishing worldwide in

Oxford New York

Athens Auckland Bangkok Bogotá Buenos Aires Calcutta
Cape Town Chennai Dar es Salaam Delhi Florence Hong Kong Istanbul
Karachi Kuala Lumpur Madrid Melbourne Mexico City Mumbai
Nairobi Paris São Paulo Singapore Taipei Tokyo Toronto Warsaw
and associated companies in Berlin Ibadan

Oxford is a registered trade mark of Oxford University Press
in the UK and certain other countries

Published in the United States
by Oxford University Press Inc., New York

© Andrew Gurr and Mariko Ichikawa 2000

The moral rights of the author have been asserted
Database right Oxford University Press (maker)

First published 2000

British Library Cataloguing in Publication Data
Data available

Library of Congress Cataloging in Publication Data

Gurr, Andrew.
    Staging in Shakespeare's theatres / Andrew Gurr and Mariko Ichikawa.
    (Oxford Shakespeare topics)
    Includes bibliographical references and index.
    1. Shakespeare, William, 1564–1616—Stage history—To 1625.
    2. Shakespeare, William, 1564–1616—Stage history—England—London.
    3. Theater—England—Production and direction—History—16th
century.   4. Theater—England—Production and direction—
History—17th century.   5. Shakespeare, William, 1564–1616—
Dramatic production.   6. Theaters—England—London—History—16th
century.   7. Theaters—England—London—History—17th century.
I. Ichikawa, Mariko.   II. Title.   III. Series.
PR3095.G88 2000 792.9′5—dc21 99–41378
ISBN 0-19-871159-X
ISBN 0-19-871158-1 (pbk.)

3 5 7 9 10 8 6 4 2

Typeset by Kolam Information Services Pvt Ltd, Pondicherry, India
Printed in Great Britain on acid-free paper by Biddles Ltd, www.Biddles.co.uk

Contents

Illustrations

Acknowledgements

Our thanks for help in the work that lies behind this book are due to Alan C. Dessen, Charles Edelman, Gabriel Egan, Frank Hildy, Pauline Kiernan, Paul Nelsen, John Orrell, Raymond Powell, Mark Rylance, Leslie Thomson, and especially to Stanley Wells, general and supervisory editor for this volume in the series. Thanks is a singular word that cannot possibly cover the multitude of goodnesses from which we have drawn the benefit. The inevitable errors and misleading speculations are our own.

The Conditions of Original Staging

a. Performance Versus Page

Shakespeare and his fellow-playwrights wrote their scripts for stages and audiences that were very different from what we are used to now. As writers for those remote stages they saw their scripts not as words to be read on the page but to be spoken, delivered as a means of telling a story through dialogue and action. What they expected from the forms of 'action', the process of acting out the narrative, was embodied in the scripts they wrote for the playing companies. Whereas a modern audience at a cinema could expect a gesture to 'yonder mountain' to be accompanied by a picture of the real thing, Elizabethans would see the speaker's gesture as an indication of where it was assumed to be, but would also know that the reference directed them to imagine something that was not there. Piecing out, as the Prologue to *Henry V* suggests, the deficiencies of the stage setting ('our imperfections') through the imagination ('with your thoughts', 23), was an automatic expectation in both writers and their audiences. Elizabethan staging was symbolic rather than realistic. Audiences had to work at visualizing the spectacles the words described. Unless we can bring to their words a fairly distinct idea of what they and their authors expected, we lose much that was inherent in their scripts.

Some indicators in the texts we read are evident signifiers, but many others are hidden or camouflaged for us now by our expectations based on modern staging or cinema. When in *Richard II*, 2.3.4,[1] Northumberland gestures at 'these high wild hills' of the Cotswolds we know he is telling his audience that the characters have been on their travels and have reached Gloucestershire. When a little later Northumberland's son refers to 'yon lime and stone' (3.3.26) of Flint Castle, we can tell fairly easily that his author expected him to gesture at the *frons scenae*, the wall at the back of the Elizabethan platform stage with its doors that the players entered by, the balcony where Romeo found Juliet, and where in *Richard II* just after Percy has identified the castle the king himself appears. It is much less easy, though, to identify what pressure Elizabethans would have felt when they saw Richard appear on the stage balcony. Physically elevated above the stage platform, the balcony signified the king's superiority over his people. This elevation he loses when he descends to the stage level, which he calls the 'base court', where Bullingbrook and the other rebels stand. That degradation Richard admits in his words. But for Elizabethans the stage balcony was also associated with more general breaches of social order, and with conquest, especially in battle-scenes where the *frons* represented a city's defensive walls and the central opening below was the city gates through which the victors march, as in *Henry V*'s siege of Harfleur.[2] As king, Richard is besieged by his people, who force him to descend to their level. For Elizabethans the staging signified a political act more potent than we can get from modern staging, which may lose the original signifiers like the king's crown and the carefully decorous behaviour of his courtiers. Before he appears on the stage balcony, Richard has already conceded his loss of status when he tells his followers to put their hats on in his presence and sit on the ground with him. In an age which has forgotten the decorums that laid down the proper behaviour in the presence of one's sovereign we lose the peculiar force that lies behind such incidents.

Without knowing something about the routine physical features of the original stages, and the expectations set in the minds of the early audiences, these allusive signals pass us by. This book will begin with an account of the physical features of the main kinds of Elizabethan playhouse, before going on to describe the more mobile devices used in the telling of the plays' stories on stage, and then to summarize this information through a detailed account of how one play, *Hamlet*, might have been staged at the Globe in 1601. Chapters 4, 5, and 6 analyse one specific and yet routine activity: the business of players entering and making their exits from the stage. Even that apparently simple action can prove to be a much more complex and intricate business than anyone who discovers their Shakespeare from a chair in a study has any reason to expect.

b. Playgoing in 1600

First, though, what would a playgoer in London have encountered when Shakespeare's plays were first staged? For Elizabethans the opening of a play was a public event, and an act of choice which had an almost religious dimension. Up to three thousand people paid to have themselves shut into a large wood-framed auditorium, expecting to spend two or three hours of their afternoon enjoying a game or play of illusion. They came to watch a fiction, the acting out of a story which they would witness, well aware of the novelty and the religious doubts about the choice they had made in observing an act designed explicitly to deceive them, willing to suspend their disbelief while they sat or stood in varying kinds of discomfort. Religious doubt about playgoers submitting to vice was more than a matter of Puritanical hostility to ordinary pleasures. In strict Church of England theology any act of deception or false illusion was said to be the work of the Devil. All playgoers were guilty of willingly consenting to be deceived, and players were accused of being agents of the Devil in their work of deception and illusion. Every playgoer would have that warning in his or her mind when they chose to pay to be entertained. The fact that they paid for the experience shows that they were all there willingly. How many of them really were concerned to 'mind true things by what their mockeries be', as the audience at the Globe in the summer of 1599 was invited to do,[3] or how many went only for mindless pleasure, we cannot tell. Their experience was certainly a lot less comfortable, less passive, more energized, than most modern playgoing. And they could not forget that it was a mockery they would see. It was easy to remain aware of what you were really doing when you were part of a noisy crowd in an uncomfortable open-air playhouse. Whether in sun or rain, everyone was visible to one another as they gathered round the stage platform where the players were about to perform. It was likely to be a harmonious if expectant public gathering. Everyone was there for the same purpose, anticipating the same things, and everyone knew their place in the playgoing community.

Before the play began the stage platform stood empty, an open and therefore inviting space in the centre of a crowd. It was not railed off, but its height, at five feet above the yard level where everyone stood around it, was enough to keep it uninvaded. Normally it was strewn with green rushes, like any indoor space in a Tudor house. Even to an inexperienced playgoer its emptiness in the heart of the crowd would have made it the focus of attention, the centre of the circle of spectators. From the standers in the yard to the nobles in their boxes on the stage balcony, people surrounded it completely. Wherever you stood or sat, you were never more than thirty-five feet from the stage platform, and most people were much closer, but from every position you could see most of the other gazers and gapers on the far side of the stage platform. It was a self-conscious grouping. You were a part of what Hamlet called 'this distracted globe', set in your own social niche, paying for your mind to be distracted briefly from the real things outside.

A good proportion of the audience was as colourfully painted as the stage, distracting as well as distracted. Clothing, from hats to footwear, reflected social status. The richer a playgoer was, the more colourful and visibly expensive was his or her dress. Status dictated the choice of fabric as well as its colour. The Sumptuary Laws, which had been established under Henry VIII to determine social rankings, were never very carefully obeyed, and were in fact abolished in 1604. But their very existence tempted social climbers to flout them, and they gave rise to numerous charges of overdressing and false exhibitionism. These were comparable to what the preachers accused stageplayers of doing, which included the idea that their deceptions licensed them to promote deceit by dressing above their true social station. Church courts not infrequently fined citizens for wearing velvet, satins or feathers, fabrics reserved for the gentry. Gold was reserved for the nobility who normally chose to sit in the lords' rooms. London citizens in the middle galleries wore blue, as did their house servants, while courtiers wore red, and gallants wore all kinds of colour. In the yard, artisans and apprentices generally dressed drably, in woollen jerkins and bonnets, some with the leather aprons of the handicraft trades.[4] Headgear reflected the level of social elevation of the wearer. Everyone wore a hat, indoors and out, and the higher the crown or feather the more insistently the hat signalled an elevated status. The artisan's woollen cap, required from 1574 by one of those pieces of government legislation designed to emphasize social distinctions and in the process help the ailing wool trade, was the characteristic mark of the groundling in the yard. In the galleries citizens and merchants wore felt hats with high crowns and small feathers. In the upper rooms and the bays of the galleries closest to the stage gallants and nobles wore higher hats with bigger feathers, possibly even an ostrich plume. It did not pay to seat yourself behind such a gallant. The exclusive status of the lords' rooms, where a noble might hire a whole box for himself and his lady or his friends, may have saved some hats from having their plumes plucked or snipped with a knife by the playgoers trapped behind them.

If you had a poor or obstructed view, however, you could move. Apart from the different prices for different parts of the auditorium, the system offered no restrictions. Once you had paid the 'gatherer' the price for entering your section of the auditorium you could go anywhere you chose. There were no designated or numbered seats. If the play attracted a large crowd everyone just had to squeeze more closely together. As in any crowd on its feet, the yard was free for people to get the best view they could. If you found yourself in an obstructed position you tried to move to a position giving you a better view. In general, the first-comers could serve themselves best, whether by taking their places on the front benches of the galleries nearest the stage or the prime standing places in the yard. Moving around the yard was routine, and not only for the playgoers. Peddlers, selling water or beer, fruit, and nuts, walked through the yard and through such of the galleries as allowed them enough space throughout the play, so long as they did not let the players hold their attention. A snide reference in Overbury's *Characters* (1614) speaks of 'a *Water-bearer* on the floore of a *Play-house*' gaping in worship of 'a wide-mouth'de *Player*'.[5]

Selling food and drink during the performance was one of the many menial jobs open to aspirant players who could not get taken on as hired men to play the non-speaking parts. Several playhouse employees were on hand while the play ran. The 'gatherers', the men or women who took the money at the doors, were the first a playgoer would encounter. Peddlers in the yard selling food were probably next, so long as the trumpeter heralding the play remained invisible on his height above the yard as he signalled to the world outside the theatre that the play was about to begin. The stage itself had its attendants, blue-coated servants who would open doors for the players with noble parts, and who would draw back the hangings from the central opening for any 'discovery'.

On the day of performance, playbills put up on posts all over the city announced and described the play that was to be performed. The standard starting-time at the Globe was two o'clock in the afternoon, though other playhouses tended to have later starts. As the time for the play drew near, a flag was hoisted up the playhouse mast, and the trumpeter on his height blew to hasten latecomers. Most of the playgoers lived in or around the city on the north side of the river, so the wealthier hired wherries and were rowed across to a wharf located barely a hundred yards from the theatre. The poorer walked over London Bridge, passed the church which is now Southwark Cathedral and then went the three hundred muddy yards along Maiden Lane to the theatre. In 1600 or 1601, when *Hamlet* was first staged, coaches for the conveyance of the rich were still a rare novelty, although gentry who lived south of the river might well arrive on horseback.

Everyone entering the playhouse focused on the empty stage and the curtained stage wall or *frons scenae* with its entry doors, waiting for the three knocks that announced the prologue or the arrival of the players on stage for the first scene. The *frons* was the face of the 'tiring house' where the actors dressed or attired themselves, using their playing costumes to give themselves the illusion of a social rank that seemed to locate them well above their officially-recognized status of servants to the nobility. Its heavily decorated and painted face had classical pilasters and carved statuary—satyrs, and probably at balcony level the figures of Thalia and Melpomene, the muses of comedy and tragedy. At the highest level nearest the 'heavens' or cover over the stage were the Gods. The Muses, figures who mediated between the Gods and the earth, occupied the middle position, while the stage level was for humanity. On each side at stage level in the *frons* was an entry door. The central opening was concealed behind a hanging or elaborate cloth woven in panels with pictures of scenes from classical myths. This cloth of 'arras' which concealed the central opening, through which Hamlet stabs Polonius, was a heavy tapestry weave. The central hangings were only used by the players for special entrances. They concealed a wide alcove, sometimes now called the 'discovery space' because of its use for special displays and shows that were 'discovered' or revealed by drawing apart the hangings. The caskets in *The Merchant of Venice*, the gold treasure which Volpone worships at the beginning of Jonson's play, the spectacle of the Duchess of Malfi's murdered children, or Faustus's study (with the 'Doctor', uncovered by the Prologue, seen sitting at a table, with book, candle and possibly a skull on it) were typical set-pieces designed to be revealed to all (except the lords sitting on the balcony over the stage) when the stage-hands drew back the hangings.

One especially colourful feature of the *frons* was its upper-level balcony positioned over the two flanking doors and the central hangings. The richest spectators sat there, the object of all eyes. They might not be able to see the 'discoveries', but they had the most conspicuous seats in the house, and they had a clear overview and better hearing of the stage action than anyone else. They were gentry, people who gave all their time to leisure. They might smoke tobacco, play cards, or simply show off their grand clothing, dress of a quality and social cachet noticeably better than the clothes the players wore when they had to counterfeit the same kind of status. For the spectator in the yard the stage balcony was where, as the playwright John Marston's cousin Everard Guilpin put it, you can 'See . . . him yonder, who sits o're the stage, | With the Tobacco-pipe now at his mouth'.[6] It was the place for the gallant, the earl, or the ambassador and his party. In later years, once Shakespeare's company acquired the Blackfriars and its famous consort of musicians, the central room on the stage balcony was curtained off and occupied by the musicians. In the earlier years, when *Hamlet* first appeared, if the play had a balcony scene the central room might be empty unless there was a distinct shortage of elevated places. If the throng of grandees was large and demanding enough it would still serve as a lords' room, whether or not the players needed it. Juliet must have been obliged many times to call her regret that Romeo had such a name from amongst a gathering of decidedly visible grandees. For *Hamlet* the balcony was not needed, and the whole of that level above the stage could have been filled with the rich and the great, as shown in a Dutch visitor's drawing of the Swan playhouse on Bankside in 1596.[7]

c. Relative Positionings in the Auditorium

The distinctive character of the auditorium had some notable side-effects which influenced both the staging and the acting. Socially the most important customers were behind and above the stage, while the lowest level was around what today we think of as the front. It was a steeply vertical sociology. This raises such questions as whether the modern terminology, front-stage and backstage, is at all appropriate. Neither is a Shakespearian term. There is still no word either in theatre language or geometry to describe the standard viewing position in a circular auditorium. We know that 'upstage' and 'downstage' were terms invented later for proscenium-arch theatres with their raked stages, so they have no meaning at the Globe. Where is the 'front' of a circle, even one with such a vertical wall and a focal stage?

The modern use of the concept of a 'front' to the stage reflects a basic change in audience thinking since 1601. The term 'audience' itself, taken from the Latin 'audire', to hear, indicates the expectation that plays are things to be heard rather than seen. In Shakespeare's time the alternative word 'spectator', from the Latin 'spectare', to see or watch, became a late intrusion which never succeeded in capturing the concept of what a playgoer truly was. Hearing is possible all around a speaker, and it is natural for an audience listening to a speech to group themselves all around him. Spectacle by contrast presupposes a frontal view, and spectators expect to group themselves in front of the picture. Modern audiences are more properly spectators, and group themselves where they expect to get the best view of the stage spectacle. Elizabethans would not have positioned themselves anything like so readily at the 'front' of the stage for a play.

The Inigo Jones drawings for an indoor playhouse (see Fig. 3), probably the Cockpit of 1616,[8] with its boxes flanking the stage and its degrees for equally privileged seating flanking the central music room on the balcony, rather more closely reflect the Globe's auditorium apart from the yard than we usually allow. They certainly affirm the grouping of the socially elevated around the sides and 'back' of the stage. So which way or ways did the actors usually face? Would it have been normal at the Swan and the Globe for the players to place themselves with their backs to their best customers? At the Swan

Johannes De Witt (see Fig. 1) showed them in the position most familiar to us, at what we call the 'front' of the stage, the lady and her waiting-woman sitting facing the crowd in the yard, and her steward making his dutiful bow to her from even closer to the under-standers at the 'front'. But even that is dubious as evidence. De Witt's drawing is of a linear staging, and apart from the depth of its square platform on which the figures stand and its concern to feature the main architectural elements, it might have done for a proscenium-arch

Figure 1. The Swan theatre, as copied from Johannes de Witt's drawing made in 1596 by his friend Arendt van Buchell in Amsterdam. It is now held in the Library of the Rijksuniversiteit, Utrecht. The *frons scenae* is notable for the absence of any curtains and for its two entry doors, both of which have been called in question.

stage. Paper is two-dimensional, whatever use we try to make of perspective when drawing on it. The *Roxana* and *Messallina* illustrations of the 1630s[9] use the same disposition, influenced though they may have been by Continental and proscenium kinds of theatre. Speeches in the plays which say something like 'Here comes X' must be taken to imply that the speakers are facing the stage entrances at the 'back' of the platform. When in *Romeo and Juliet* 3.5 the first quarto's stage direction says '*She lookes after Nurse*', Juliet was clearly meant to watch the Nurse make her exit, and therefore to face the *frons scenae*. Of course, this might also be taken to imply that the boy playing Juliet would normally have been expected to face the yard, and that the stage direction was necessary in order to ensure that he did the opposite at this moment. But three-dimensional acting makes it wrong to think of any 'normal' direction to look in. Acting in the round requires a non-linear positioning, facing in whatever direction the action requires.

This question impacts strongly on the business of where actors chose to stand on the stage, and where or who they faced. The 'front' edge of the Globe's stage was positioned at the centre of the circle of audience, and it might be expected that choruses, soliloquies and other speeches directly addressed to the audience would be spoken from there. But from that centre the speaker might face in any one or more directions round the circle of audience. Whether they really did position themselves at the stage edge, and whether there was any special significance in the other possible positions on the stage is not yet clearly understood. Medieval staging, the tradition out of which the first London theatres like the Globe evolved, sometimes used a concept that ultimately stemmed from classical Roman theatre. Roman stages had a massive *frons*, an elaborate back wall stretching across a stage which was much broader than the London types. The position close to the entry-points in the *frons* was known as the *locus*, the place of authority, while the open spaces closer to the audience stood for the *platea*, the street or any other common place where ordinary folk went about their usually comic business. Recently it has been suggested[10] that the two equivalent positions on Tudor stages had a similar significance. Court scenes, official hearings in the royal presence, for instance, conducted with the king sitting on his throne in judgement, would call for a throne on its three-step dais to be placed by the stage hands fairly close to the *frons*, though not actually backed up against it, looking 'forward' towards the yard. It may well have been normally positioned over the stage trap, on the centre line but rather nearer the *frons* than the yard. The carpentry of the trap most likely made foot-falls on it sound rather different from the rest of the stage, so there was a distinct gain to be made by placing any large properties there to avoid the change in sound as someone walked over it.

Such a positioning was not quite the same as the medieval *locus*, but a location near the mid-stage certainly suited the Globe stage's design. All subordinate characters would stand facing the throne (it was dangerously disrespectful to turn your back on royalty), the men with their hats in their hands. If they addressed the king they would kneel at the foot of the dais. The fact that this meant most of the characters on stage had to face inwards, away from the throng in the yard, was incidental. They confronted the on-stage authority figure, and in the process they also faced the audience's 'lords' who chose to sit on the balcony.

That is what current thinking suggests: it is quite possible, however, that we have been misled by our unfamiliarity with Elizabethan staging practices, after several centuries of proscenium-arch staging with all the characters routinely facing the front where all the audience are clustered, a convention now intensified by cinema screens. The Tudor emphasis on status and place makes it conceivable that the throne was usually positioned facing the lords, not the groundlings. If so, it would have occupied what Robert Weimann identifies as the *platea*, the ordinary street area, not the authority position of tradition. That is considered unlikely, except in special circumstances such as one central scene in *Hamlet*, which we shall come to later. The authority position was most likely close to the *frons*, facing what we think of as forwards, or to the 'front' of the stage. If indeed it was there, the consequent associations of *locus* and *platea* may have had a more positive role to play in the original staging than we can easily recognize today.

d. Playgoing Minds

This brief and summary account of the conditions under which an Elizabethan playgoer would have experienced a play says very little about what would have been in their minds, and not very much about their likely knee-jerk reactions to the various incidents. No two play-goers have the same experience, however similar their training and their positions in the auditorium. There are simply no forms of record even for modern playgoing that are adequate to create more than a minimal identification of how a play in performance affected its audience. Anyone who reads a review of a play they have just seen, or reads one of the 'plays in performance' books which try to describe how a particular play was staged or filmed, knows how variable the experience of a play as an event can be. This book suffers the same problem. It tries to augment the only means of recording performances that the Elizabethans had, the play-text itself, with as much ancillary information about the playing conditions, along with the mindsets of the players and the playgoers, as can be filtered from the sketchy fragments of material evidence. It can only be successful in raising consciousness about some of the details that do not readily manifest themselves in the text itself. It will use the text, that two-dimensional bird who sits on brood over the deep Shakespearian mysteries, in an attempt to identify some of the details forming the third dimension, a realization of the text in its original performance conditions. It will aim at identifying the typical rather than the exceptional, those routine features that were an integral part of the rich Elizabethan playgoing heritage that we have lost. As an essential accompaniment to that, it will also try to show how such three-dimensionality can illuminate some of the hidden elements in the texts that we think we know so well already.

The two-dimensional written text differed from the three dimensions of the performed text as it was staged in many ways. Few of the elements that were inherent in the early staging can be identified now with much confidence. Just one illustration of the difference between the two-dimensional written text and the three dimensions of staging can be cited here: the practice of doubling parts in the early perform-ances. *Julius Caesar* has parts for nine main speakers of the men's roles, two for women, and eleven minor speaking parts, a total of twenty-three characters (twenty men, three women and a boy), not counting several unnamed citizens, attendants, and soldiers.[11] Thomas Platter saw it performed at the Globe on 21 September 1599, by a total of what he counted as fifteen players. The fifteen he identified obviously shared all twenty-three speaking parts between them, plus the crowd scenes. Doubling was a routine practice. *Henry V,* staged shortly before *Julius Caesar,* has forty-two parts, all of which would have been taken by the same fifteen players. A player taking more than one role must have been easily recognizable in any other, since Platter was confident of his count. A change of clothing, even just a new hat, was probably enough to identify a change of character.

Doubling offered rich possibilities for metatheatrical games. The *Henry V* staged at the new Globe's first season in 1997 was done with an all-male cast of fifteen. The player of Fluellen also took the part of Le Fer, so that he had Pistol threatening him at Agincourt as a neat contrast to his browbeating of Pistol before and after the battle. The conspirators in France's pay in Act 2 became French gallants two scenes later. The player of the Dauphin in the early scenes became the Dauphin's mother in Act 5. Metatheatricality ruled. Some games of this kind were written into the texts by the author. If Richard Burbage as the leading player of Shakespeare's company played Richard II, the sun-king who sets in that play, he would probably also have played Prince Hal in its sequel, and promised to rise again through the Falstaffian clouds, using the identical image:

> Yet herein will I imitate the sun,
> Who doth permit the base contagious clouds
> To smother up his beauty from the world.

So the dead sun-king rises again in the person of the doubling player, and the son of the usurper will shine like the lawful king whom his father deposed. Tudor minds were set on the truths that shone through theatrical illusion. Stage realism was a lower priority to them than such half-hidden metatheatrical and metaphysical truths.

e. A Short History of Professional Playing in London

The conditions of playgoing for entertainment changed substantially in London through even the relatively brief period of Shakespeare's working life there. He spent the twenty years of his maturity working in London and profiting from his plays and his share in his acting company. By the time he retreated to Stratford in 1609 or after, he had witnessed and helped to shape a colourful transformation of London life. But even such a radical and rapid transformation took time, and as a part of the context for the plays it is essential to register the changes in the forms of London playgoing and staging through that period. These changes profoundly affected the theatres, the playing companies, their status, and their organization as much as the repertories for which the companies bought their stock of playbooks. Some idea of the historical context in London before and after the period of Shakespeare's working life is an essential accompaniment to the story of how the Elizabethans and Jacobeans staged their plays.

Playgoing was still a novelty when Shakespeare first came to London in the late 1580s. In the early years of the Reformation several different cultural traditions began to cross-fertilize each other and to evolve in new forms. In London the process gradually came to mean that a playgoing Londoner could expect to be able to see a different play each afternoon, staged either at a city inn or in a purpose-built playhouse designed for Londoners' common entertainment. From that decade onwards Court, city, and country traditions began to merge in London. With Shakespeare and Marlowe as their spearhead the professional companies started a tradition that catered for all tastes in England. It was a tradition that Parliament stopped abruptly in 1642, at the beginning of its long war with the crown for authority. Since then it has covered the world.

The new tradition began to settle down in the years around 1590. From 1594 any Londoner could enjoy the unique privilege created by the Privy Council. As the central committee of government it granted licences for two professional acting companies to perform daily in London's suburbs, one in Shoreditch to the north and the other on the south bank of the Thames in Surrey. The official reason was that the Queen expected to be entertained, and the professional companies that played before her each Christmas needed a means to polish their skills. The reality was official endorsement for London's new habit of playgoing.

The two companies enjoyed the fruits of the quasi-monopoly this official licence gave them. They were supremely talented groups culled from the best players in the country. One company was graced with all the Marlowe plays, the other with all the earlier Shakespeares, comedies such as *The Comedy of Errors*, *The Taming of the Shrew* and *The Two Gentlemen of Verona*, history plays including the *Henry VI* sequence and *Richard III*, and tragedies like *Titus Andronicus* and possibly *Romeo and Juliet*, together with the new resources promised by the man himself as player and writer.

From 1594 onwards these two companies, their patrons leading members of the Privy Council—Charles Howard, the Lord Admiral, and Henry Carey, the Lord Chamberlain—did more than any other group to exploit the new fashion in plays and the new security the Privy Council gave them. They had many advantages. One was the number of unemployed university graduates trying to eke out a living in London by writing. More potent than that was the intensity of the demand laid on such writers by the new playhouses in the suburbs and the new companies using them. The large number of Londoners and visitors to the city who flocked to this novel entertainment of professionally staged plays developed an appetite which demanded constant change. With only two companies performing regularly you could not run a new play for long without losing your audiences. In fact, as we know from the day-by-day records of the plays staged at the Rose on Bankside between 1592 and 1600, the companies soon got into the habit of staging a different play every single day.[12] At the Rose the Admiral's Men performed as many as forty different plays a year, in a repertory that called on them to perform every afternoon for six days a week. They never ran the same play on successive days. Some plays did not outrun their first performance, and even the most popular were not staged more than four times in any one month.

That was hard on the players, but it fed a vast appetite which the new writers, including the grammar-school-educated man from the country, Shakespeare, had to satisfy. The very innovativeness of new plays like *Tamburlaine*, *Dr Faustus*, and *The Jew of Malta* helped to create its own fresh demands, above all for constant novelty. Sequels and imitations of the most popular plays there certainly were, but even they had to match the new standards, in particular a more ambitious size of cast and spectacular modes of staging. A fresh kind of play, written to be staged with greater resources than ever before, sprang into being in the late 1580s to feed the audiences at the new playhouses.

For the two privileged companies set up in 1594 the later 1590s were a time of unprecedented success and consolidation. In their different ways both companies settled down to the system the Lord Chamberlain established for them. Towards the end of the century, after some complex manoeuvring that involved them exchanging places between one side of London and the other, each company created its own new playhouse to the design that their acting tradition required.[13]

In 1594 the Lord Chamberlain and his son-in-law, the Lord Admiral, assigned them to play at the Rose on the Surrey bank of the Thames and the Theatre in Shoreditch to the north. The Lord Chamberlain, responsible for the regulation of the professional playing companies, set up Richard Burbage and his company at Burbage's father's playhouse, the Theatre, with Shakespeare and his plays. The Lord Chamberlain's son-in-law set up Edward Alleyn and his company at Alleyn's father-in-law's playhouse, the Rose, with a repertory that included almost all of the dead Marlowe's plays. For the next six years these two companies enjoyed a near-monopoly of performing in London. They were the only companies chosen to perform at court each Christmas, and the durability of their tenure in London, freed from the need to travel the country for most of the year, brought them an unprecedented level of income.

The Admiral's Men played at the Rose on Bankside for the next six years, but the Chamberlain's Men had a less happy time with their playhouse. The lease of the land on which the Theatre was built ran out in April 1597, and when it expired the site's owner promptly ejected the players and the playhouse closed. James Burbage as the Theatre's owner had expected this to happen, and had other plans. Through 1596 he had been building a new playhouse, inside the city itself, in the Blackfriars precinct just below St Paul's. The precinct was a 'liberty', inside the city and yet free from the Lord Mayor's control. Burbage bought part of a large and ancient hall, stripping it of its partitions to make a roofed and enclosed hall theatre. Evidently his plan was to abandon playing in the suburbs to which the Lord Mayor's hostility had relegated them and to give his company an enclave that returned them to a central part of the city, but one where the Lord Mayor's authority did not extend.

It was an ingenious concept, and one which might well have made the open-air suburban playhouses redundant forty years before they finally expired. Unfortunately as a vision of the future of London playgoing it proved premature. The Blackfriars precinct was a wealthy neighbourhood, home to many influential figures, including the Lord Chamberlain himself and his Revels Office which controlled the professional companies. In November 1596 a petition signed by 140 of the Blackfriars inhabitants was presented to the Privy Council demanding to have the playhouse stopped. They won, and two months later Burbage died, leaving his sons to secure what they could out of the mess he left them. The Theatre's lease was about to expire, and in April the playhouse was closed. For the next two years the Lord Chamberlain's Men had to play their repertory, by now including *The Merchant of Venice, Richard II* and *1 Henry IV* and the other Falstaff plays, in the adjacent Curtain playhouse which they rented. Meanwhile Richard and Cuthbert Burbage, committed to financing the company as heirs to James Burbage's various properties including the unusable new Blackfriars playhouse, tried to negotiate a new deal with the owner of the Theatre's site.

They had made no progress by Christmas 1598. So they contracted a builder to pull the Theatre down and transport its framing timbers to a new site on Bankside, barely fifty yards from the Rose, on a thirty-five year lease, and set out to build a new playhouse, which they later named the Globe.[14] This was quickly done, though the irate owner of the Theatre's site sued the builder for trespass and charged the Burbages with stealing the timbers. The Globe grew in 1599 in a flurry of legal charges and a distinct shortage of cash. The savings incurred by re-using the Theatre's timbers allowed the two Burbages to put up half the cost of the new playhouse, but for the other half they needed more help. Since the other players in the company had a strong interest in getting a new playhouse, the Burbages turned to them. Shakespeare and three of his colleagues put up the balance of the cost of the Globe. Thus five of the company's leading players, Richard Burbage included, were turned into co-landlords, with the company as a whole their tenants.

This novel merger of tenant and landlord proved a uniquely happy arrangement. To some extent it must have reflected the working system which the playing companies had evolved for themselves, where eight or more of the chief players shared in the company's work and fortunes. In a deeply authoritarian and status-conscious age this was a remarkably co-operative and democratic system. As 'sharers' working in a co-operative system, about which more will be said below, the Lord Chamberlain's Men must have been outstandingly good at teamwork.

Not surprisingly, Henslowe and Alleyn at the Rose were unhappy with the location of their new neighbours. The bigger playhouse now looming next door to the Rose on Bankside prompted them to move in the opposite direction. They built the Fortune playhouse in Clerkenwell, a suburb to the north of the city, using the same builder who had just completed the Globe, but making it square in contrast to the Rose and the Globe's near-circular polygons. Both sets of impresarios secured the Privy Council's blessing for the exchange of locations.

f. The Great Years

The first ten years for the two chosen companies at their new playhouses, the Globe and the Fortune, were as prosperous as they had been in the first three years up to 1597. But it was now less easy to maintain their pre-eminence, and the competition grew. Two companies comprising boy players, modelled on the chorister companies that had been closed down in 1590, started up in a new form, one at a small indoor theatre attached to St Paul's Cathedral, the other using the hall in the Blackfriars owned by the Burbages but barred from any use by companies of adult players. A third adult company forced its way into London too, playing at a converted inn just outside the city walls to the east in Stepney. When King James came from Scotland to the English throne after Elizabeth's death he endorsed the players' status in the city by making his own family patrons of the three adult companies, and allowed the two boy companies to go on with their plays as well. He took the Lord Chamberlain's Men under his own wing, gave his elder son the Admiral's Men at the Fortune, and gave the third company to Queen Anne. She added the Blackfriars company of boys to her patronage, though their satirical repertory soon got them into trouble, and she had to renounce them little more than a year later.

The five years from James's accession in 1603 to the long closure brought about by a massive epidemic of plague in 1608 were healthier for the adult companies than the boys. The Fortune company matched Shakespeare's hugely popular comedies from his middle period and the new tragedies (*Hamlet, Othello, Lear, Macbeth*) with plays based on stories from Foxe's *Book of Martyrs* about England's Protestant heroes. The Queen's Men at the Red Bull started to develop a repertory full of colourful and spectacular plays full of battles, epic travels, and romance. The two boy companies, claiming a superior social status with their small, roofed theatres and the privilege of freedom from censorship by staging their plays for 'private' audiences, each went their own way. After a shaky start with some plays from the older pre-1590 repertory, Paul's Boys developed a new line in 'citizen comedy', plays about contemporary London that either directly or satirically put their focus on citizen life. The Blackfriars Boys took Ben Jonson from Shakespeare's company, and began a career in satire. They initiated what has been called the 'War of the Theatres', staging plays in which Jonson, Dekker, and Marston savaged each other for public entertainment. The Blackfriars repertory soon became notorious for its scandalous satires. After a long run in which the court and especially James's long following of Scotsmen were ridiculed, their repertory became too troublesome. In *The Isle of Gulls*, staged early in 1606, half the cast spoke with Scottish accents. During the year before *Eastward Ho!* had mocked a group of pro-citizen plays from the Paul's Boys repertory, and was censured for a sardonic reference to Scottish courtiers. During the plague closure of 1608 the Blackfriars Boys' impresario surrendered his lease of the theatre to the two Burbages, and most of the boy players moved to other companies, mainly of adults.

The belated acquisition by the Burbages in 1608 of a playhouse built by their father for their company twelve years before led to some drastic changes in the possibilities open for playgoing in London. The practices that had long pre-dated 1594, when companies coming to London would perform either at the Theatre or Curtain in the suburbs or, whenever possible, inside the city at the inns—outdoors through the better weather in innyards, and indoors in their great upper rooms in winter—could now be renewed by the one company, the King's Men. The Blackfriars, uniquely well placed inside the city, had been freed from the Privy Council's prohibition on playing through its years of use by the boy company, which had played there only once a week. Now the King's Men could play there daily through the winter, just as they remembered doing at the city's inns.

Generously, probably in the spirit of sharing and teamwork which ruled the Shakespeare company, the Burbages gave shares in their new playhouse to the players who already had shares in the Globe. The company now became landlord and tenant of the two best playing-places in London. They played through the summer at the Globe and through the winter at the Blackfriars, leaving their other venue empty, much to the envy of the other companies. That policy, self-indulgent as it was, became the ultimate mark of their pre-eminence amongst the London companies. In time the Blackfriars became the most reputable playhouse in London, frequented by the highest social strata. Even royalty went to the Blackfriars to see plays, an eminence which helped to cost the players their livelihood when the king fell from power and Parliament closed all of London's playhouses in 1642.

This is a story of rapid growth, and of a new establishment which was protected from the city's considerable hostility by royal licence. Through its seventy years of development its practices took on new forms, although the practitioners were always ruled by traditions that grew early and proved their worth through constant testing. In what follows we try to identify the main features of those traditions, and to place them, along with some of the plays that were written for them, at roughly the point of historical development where they originated.

Shakespeare's Theatres and the Evidence of the Texts

a. Playtexts and Playhouses

The nearest thing to copyright protection that operated in Shakespeare's time was not designed to give authors control over their products. Texts were still thought of principally as manuscripts, unique copies, and the only form of protection that existed was for texts that got into print. Even then the Stationers' Company, which was responsible for controlling publication in printed forms, in fact served as a monopoly company protected by the government which, in return for its privileged position, did the work of licensing and regulating the 150 or so printers based in London. Printers and booksellers paid fees to register their copy with the company. This gave them a licence to print what and when their judgement of the bookselling market indicated might be profitable. Authors had no say in this process. It was a system designed to control what was printed, and to protect the rights of printers and publishers.

Playwrights gave up all rights to their play manuscripts when they sold them to the playing companies. The plays, kept private through their uniqueness as manuscripts or 'playbooks', were reproduced by their owners only in the form of handwritten copies. Normally even transcripts would not be sold to a publisher until their initial value as copies of the unique playbook was thought to be finished. In their first existence as manuscripts, most copies were made in the form of the players' scripts, individual 'parts' or speeches with their cues for particular players to learn. As owners of these items of company property, outvalued only by the company's stock of special playing costumes, the players could do with the texts what they pleased. Various inserts and cuts were periodically made in every playbook. The allusion in *Hamlet* to the 'little eyases', the boy companies which were taking audiences from the Globe, for instance (2.2.319–46),[1] was a late addition to the acting text. The reference by the Chorus in *Henry V* (5.0.29–32) to the Queen's 'General' returning to London with the Irish rebellion impaled on his sword, a likelihood in the summer of 1599, would have had to be cut once the Earl of Essex had returned in disgrace that September and was sent to the Tower. Many local allusions must have been trimmed when their occasion passed, and new local allusions inserted as occasion called for them. The players fitted their scripts to their various occasions. They did the same with their staging.

Acting is a profession dominated by conservative practices. Small companies of players working as a team and performing in constantly changing conditions had to sustain themselves by operating under well-understood and therefore long-running traditions. Their performances had to be inherently portable, and their staging traditions reflected that need more than any other. The players had neither expectation nor experience of playing in any one venue for any length of time. Their training-grounds were the various locations where they performed on their travels: market-places, guildhalls, inns and inn-yards, church halls, and the halls of great houses.[2] When a company visited a provincial town or country house no one location could be used more than two or three times, and no play could be staged in the same location more than once. Consequently their traditions were based on the habits they learned from travelling. Plays had to be staged under whatever conditions could be found on the day of or immediately following the company's arrival in a new place. Since the best form of transport they could expect was a covered cart and a few horses for the ten or a dozen players and their equipment, everything had to be light, portable, and easily fitted to the alien circumstances. They could rarely stay more than two or three days in any one place, and the few plays they travelled with had to be adapted to a wide range of venues and resources. The essence of the traditional practices they brought to the new venues in London was versatility and adaptability. These developed as familiar acting practices and minimal staging.

After the 1570s, once plays began to be censored and licensed for performance by the Master of the Revels, the so-called 'prompt copy' or playhouse manuscript became vital because it carried his signature allowing its performance.[3] Mayors of the towns visited would demand to see it before they agreed to anything being staged under their authority. These manuscripts thus contained the fullest text that the company could perform. They could cut it, but not add to it. Such manuscripts, still known to modern play editors as 'prompt' copies, the most celebrated of which provided the long Folio text of *Hamlet*, supplied the optimum text for a performance. Editors have, however unknowingly, been trying to establish a full or optimal text, the censored and approved version that the Master of the Revels licensed, not the text that would have actually been performed. How often that optimum was realized on stage is anybody's guess. Cutting scenes that made special demands such as a trapdoor for a performance where the venue could not provide one was an obvious recourse. Trimming speeches because the full script seemed overlong or because a stand-in player of the part had to perform it was another. The Master's licence gave no allowance for adding to a text, but cutting was easy and legitimate. Whether the more than four thousand lines of the second quarto version of *Hamlet* were ever spoken even at the Globe is a question to which we can give no confident answer. The Folio text is shorter, though only by two hundred lines.

The standard length of Elizabethan performances is still a matter of some dispute. Centuries of editors, careful to restore every trace of Shakespeare's original inspiration, have fitted in every word he is thought to have written, regardless of whether it was intended for the final staged version of the play or not. The 'eclectic' text of *King Lear*, designed to incorporate everything Shakespearian from both of the early printed texts, is now thought to duplicate some of its material, since it includes both the original and the revised version. Readers of the 'eclectic' text of *Lear* are unlikely to be reading the script that was performed at the Globe. The idea that Shakespeare might have revised his work has been accepted by editors only reluctantly. *Hamlet's* fourth soliloquy, for instance ('How all occasions do inform against me'), illustrates the gradual acceptance of this idea through the 1980s. Harold Jenkins's Arden edition of 1982 included the authorial second quarto text's lead-in and the full soliloquy in his version of 4.4. Philip

Edwards in the Cambridge edition of 1984 kept it in his version, but set it in square brackets as an addendum to the Folio version, on the grounds that its information does not really fit. George Hibbard's edition in the Oxford series in 1987 included it only as a footnote.[4] It is safe to say in general that any edition prepared for the reader is likely to incorporate more of the text than was ever heard in the early performances.

The question of the performed texts being cut is a large one, and there is not much evidence about what might have been taken out of any specific performance. Cutting the playscript of course also raises the question of how long an early performance was likely to have lasted. With nearly half the early audiences watching the play on their feet, the current expectation that even a cut version of any modern Shakespeare must last for at least three hours seems out of keeping with the original conditions of performance. The great majority of claims about the length of an early performance speak like *Romeo and Juliet*'s prologue of the 'two hours traffic of the stage'. Three hours for the total stretch of the afternoon's entertainment was the maximum time that anyone ever claimed for a performance in Shakespeare's day. Playing with no intervals, the normal stretch of time identified as what people routinely paid for, including the jig that ended the performance, was two hours.[5] The odds are that originally the plays did not run nearly as long as they do in modern productions.

There were many reasons and many ways in the early period to make the speed of a performance faster than in modern theatres. There were no sets to change, and the players made no use of scene or even act breaks to create any pauses in the action. Whether they spoke their lines very much faster than modern actors is a matter for speculation, but the enthusiasm for witplay as the mind's equivalent to swordplay, and the mind's capacity to absorb modern uses of quick speech for rap or comic monologue makes it very likely. Cutting lines and scenes was standard practice, if only to fit a familiar play onto an unfamiliar stage. The players, not the authors, owned the playbooks, and they were free to cut them as they pleased or as the conditions dictated. Shakespeare may have been able to defend his own texts as a sharer in the company, but it is doubtful whether even in his own working years on the Globe's stage he succeeded in securing very many performances of the complete text of his original concept of his plays as recorded in the playbook licensed by the Master of the Revels, what the last of the Masters called the 'allowed booke'.[6]

b. The Restricted Venues

Staging had to be minimal to cope with the radical variations in the resources the companies encountered. Few of the country venues offered much more than an open space backed by either a curtained booth or one or more entry doors, usually access through a curtain stretched across the back of the acting space. The indoor venues which the travelling companies came to favour (they gave a better chance of restricting admission to those who paid at the door: in marketplaces the company was dependent on how much spectators chose to drop into the circulating hat) were the upper rooms at inns or a town's guildhall, low-roofed spaces used for drinking or, in the guildhalls, as meeting-places and civic courtrooms. Normally these indoor venues lacked the stage balcony and the central opening of the London amphitheatres, and even acting on a raised stage platform in such rooms required hasty construction of boards on trestles. Open-air innyards did offer a balcony for the players behind the temporary stage platform, as well as space around the yard's surrounding gallery to augment the crowd surrounding the stage. Guildhalls were much less generous.

The extra audience space on the elevated galleries of country inn-yards may have influenced the design of the first playhouses specially built in London, enhanced by the example of the space provided by the triple ranks of galleries in the animal-baiting houses. Several inns inside the city of London were converted for playing in the 1580s, as were inns at Bristol and York in the early 1600s when visiting players were stopped from using guildhalls. For Londoners the more advantageous location of the inns at the heart of the city offset the constant hostility exhibited by the city fathers to the early travelling companies. City inns were always favoured for playing in the 1580s and early 1590s, although they were always a much more risky venue than the Theatre, Curtain, and Rose in the suburbs. The Queen's Men, the leading company between 1583 and 1590, are on record as playing at one time or another in every one of London's playing venues, indoors and out, playhouse and inn.

The upper rooms of inns inside the city provided players with the advantage of shelter in bad weather. Their entry doors provided an even more secure system of admission than the yards of the city's inns, which was some compensation for the smaller numbers they held. A few of the inns were specifically adapted to show plays up to 1594, when the city finally secured a trade-off with the Privy Council, allowing the Theatre and the Rose to be licensed for playing in return for a ban on any playing at the city inns. The Bel Savage on Ludgate Hill below St Paul's and the Bull in Gracechurch Street running north from London Bridge turned their innyards over to playing, while the Bell and the Cross Keys in Gracechurch Street seem to have had upper rooms used for indoor playing. The Bel Savage's scaffolding of galleries, presumably a jerry-built extension of the original inn structure, was severely shaken by an earthquake in 1580. The Bankside Beargarden's scaffolding collapsed while people were watching a baiting there on a Sunday in January 1583, killing several spectators and prompting an outcry about the sin of going to see plays or baitings. John Field, father of a famous boy player who later joined the King's Men, wrote a furious pamphlet called *A godly exhortation, by occasion of the late judgement of God, shewed at Parris-garden, the thirteenth day of Januarie: where were assembled by estimation above a thousand persons, whereof some were slaine.*[7]

The first of the open-air amphitheatres was built in the eastern suburb of Stepney in 1567 by James Burbage's brother-in-law John Brayne, and called the Red Lion. Nothing is known about what was staged at it, but its successor the Theatre, financed by Brayne and Burbage in Shoreditch by one of the main roads north in 1576, soon became a notable resource for the Devil's work of staging plays. Another built at almost the same time at Newington Butts in Surrey on the road south, a mile from London Bridge, was a smaller affair, and seems to have been used only when for one reason or another the other venues were not available. The two new companies created by the Privy Council in May 1594 spent a week playing there before they separated and started their long runs at the Theatre and the Rose. A fourth early playhouse, the Curtain, built near the Theatre, was overshadowed by its neighbour and never became as celebrated, even though Shakespeare's company staged *Romeo and Juliet* and the first performances of *1 Henry IV*, *The Merry Wives of Windsor*, and *Much Ado* there in 1597–8 while they looked for a new playhouse. In 1614 it was rated the worst place for plays in London. By then it had become the longest-lasting of all the amphitheatres, and was still used into the 1620s. The Globe and the Fortune, the most famous and durable of all the Shakespearian venues, both burned down and had to be rebuilt, but even their doubled existence was shorter than the Curtain's.

All of these outdoor venues shared the same basic features. These were essentially a circuit or square of scaffolding forming galleries which usually comprised three levels of seating capable of holding up to two thousand people. The space in their yards admitted half as many again, which meant that the biggest venues were capable of admitting as many as three thousand customers. Shapes and dimensions varied widely. The innyard theatres and two later buildings converted into playhouses from inns, the Boar's Head in Whitechapel and the Red Bull in Clerkenwell, along with the Fortune, which was built to be comparable to and yet manifestly different from the round Globe, were square. The exterior walls of the Fortune made an eighty-foot square. The Theatre and Curtain, the Rose, the Swan, and the Globe all tried to make themselves circular, which given the cost of constructing oak frame timbers in circular form meant building a many-sided polygon. The Rose had fourteen sides, the Theatre and the Globe probably twenty, and the Swan possibly twenty-four. The Rose's diameter was about seventy-four feet, while the others seem to have been nearer one hundred.

These quasi-amphitheatrical structures, modelled at some remove on the Roman theatres, had galleries divided into segments or 'bays' of roughly the same size, sixteen or so feet at the rear, twelve at the front, and ten and a half feet front to back. The Rose had fourteen bays, the Globe and the Fortune twenty. Each bay had rows of benches or 'degrees' for the sitters ranked up from the balusters that edged the yard. The stages projected into the yard from the players' dressing room or 'tiring house'. The Rose's stage was tapered, much wider than it was long, forming an elongated hexagon, but those at the Swan, the Globe, and the Fortune seem to have been square. All yards were open to the sky, to give ample light, but the stages were covered, to protect the players' prime asset, their costumes, from wet weather. The stage cover, known as the 'shadow' or 'heavens', was upheld by two large columns which rose from near the front of the stage. These, painted at the Swan and probably at the others to look like classical marble columns, were the most prominent feature of the whole stage platform, apart from the painting around the entrance doors and across the *frons scenae* or tiring-house front.

The first three durable outdoor constructions in 1576–77 were matched by a pair of indoor venues, the first two of London's five hall theatres built before 1660. Some of the schools, such as the Merchant Taylors, had been using their halls for plays performed for money through the preceding decades. But authority frowned on even the performance of plays for ostensibly educational purposes. School performances depended on a single enthusiastic schoolmaster persuading his masters that acting was good training in speech and rhetoric. The commercial backing to this impulse appeared in 1576 when two playhouses were built for boy companies who as a diversion from their chorister work had been staging plays to raise money for their master. For one, a small playhouse was built onto one of the flanking bays of St Paul's, and a rather more ambitious venue was created for the other in a hall at the old Blackfriars complex. This playhouse, now known as the 'first Blackfriars', was used in the 1580s by a group formed from a merger of the two boy companies that used these indoor venues. It ran under John Lyly up to 1590, when the Privy Council closed it down.

A memory of this first Blackfriars must have lodged in James Burbage's mind in 1596, when the lease of the land on which his Theatre had been built was coming to its end and he needed a new venue. In 1594 the Privy Council had accepted the Lord Mayor's insistence that plays must be banned from performance inside the city. Being confined to play at the open-air playhouses in the suburbs through winter was evidently a pain to the companies. As the first winter of the new regime approached in October 1594 Burbage's company at the Theatre prompted their patron to request special leave from the Lord Mayor to let them play instead at the Cross Keys inside the city, an indoor venue. The Lord Chamberlain's letter has a tentative air. He took care to make it only a request, not an order, and to give heavy reassurances about the players' behaviour. It seems unlikely that this request was granted, because by the next winter Burbage was planning another way round the problem. The Blackfriars precinct, where the first hall playhouse had been, was in a 'liberty', a relic of the monastic regime which had once occupied the area, and the Lord Mayor's jurisdiction did not cover it. Officially the Lord Mayor had no control over either Paul's or the two hall playhouses built in Blackfriars because both were in liberties. So Burbage conceived the idea of constructing a new indoor playhouse also located in a liberty in the heart of the city, to replace the old open-air Theatre.

The fiasco which came out of that ingeniously imaginative plan has been described above. What the plan signified in 1596, though, was the radical preference of the leading company's impresario. He wanted a roofed theatre in a central location rather than a renewal of the amphitheatre in the suburbs which he had created twenty years before. In time his company recovered from his mistake. First a new boy company moved into the new Blackfriars in 1600. Their once-weekly performances got the inhabitants used to plays being staged there, with the result that the now royally-patronized Shakespeare company was able to start making use of it when the plague closures of 1608–10 came to an end. From then until the general closure of the playhouses in 1642 the King's Men playing at the second Blackfriars came to dominate all London playgoing.

The design of the Blackfriars and its imitators, the Cockpit or Phoenix built in 1617 in Drury Lane in the city of Westminster, and the Salisbury Court built in 1627 in the Whitefriars, also outside the city of London, was different in many ways from the older type of playhouse. The entire audience was seated, with the most expensive places closest to the stage. Even the more affluent elements among the groundlings, characterized by Jonson as a 'shop's foreman', if they could afford the higher prices, were relegated to the topmost gallery at the back of the auditorium, the place derisively known in nine-teenth-century operatic theatre as the 'gods'. This meant that the disposition of an indoor auditorium was drastically opposed in its social disposition to the groupings in the amphitheatres. Where in the popular venues the poorest were crowded in the most conspicuous positions closest to the stage, at the Blackfriars and the Cockpit they were at the rear, and the richest were closest and most visible. The Blackfriars introduced London for the first time to the general dis-position of seating that prevails in modern theatres.

Other differences were more technical. The Blackfriars had no need of stage posts, for instance, and in addition to the 'degrees' or benches

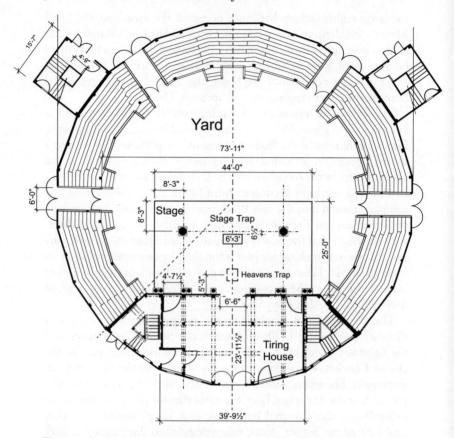

Figure 2. A plan by Jon Greenfield of Pentagram, showing the dimensions of the new Globe at Southwark at ground level.

'above' on each side of the stage balcony's central music room it had a box or boxes on each flank of the stage itself for the best places. More strikingly and much more awkwardly for the players, the smaller dimensions of the stage platform itself were constricted even further by a practice that started with the boy companies. This allowed up to fifteen gallants to collect stools from the tiring house and use them to sit on the stage itself. Although there were no stage posts, the size of the indoor stage platforms was little more than one-third that of the open-air stages. The gallants on their stools reduced that space even more.

The second Blackfriars was set up in timber inside a stone-walled hall measuring 66 feet by 46. Like the Theatre and the Globe, its three levels of wooden galleries were curved around the pit, with the 'front' edge of its stage at the centre. In every way it was a smaller, more intimate and more costly place. The physical differences between the

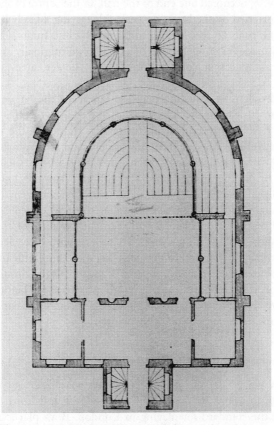

Figure 3. The ground plan by Inigo Jones, made for an indoor theatre, probably in 1616. The originals are in the library of Worcester College, Oxford. The exact scale used for the drawing is uncertain, but the outside dimension for the width of the stage with its flanking boxes for audience, for instance, was most likely intended to be 40 feet, with the width of the stage 20 feet.

two types and especially their stage space can be seen by comparing a ground plan of the Globe at yard level with Inigo Jones's ground plan which forms part of his design for an indoor theatre, very possibly the Cockpit, the first playhouse built to imitate the success of the second Blackfriars. The dimensions of the two stages are 44 feet across by 27 deep at the Globe, compared with roughly 20 feet by 16 in the Inigo Jones drawing (see Figs. 2 and 3). The Blackfriars stage, backed by its tiring house, occupied one end of the hall, in the centre of the 44-foot span, shortened by the boxes on each side, giving a likely breadth of little more than 20 feet and a similar depth. The Inigo Jones plans, probably made for an adaptation of a circular pit originally intended to contain audiences at cock-fighting shows, depict an even smaller interior.

The problem of adjusting plays designed for the larger open-air playhouses to the smaller capacities of the indoor theatres does not seem to have been very difficult for players trained in the versatility born of travelling. Making those adjustments was, in any case, chiefly a problem only for the King's Men once they started their durable practice of playing at the Globe through each summer and moving to the Blackfriars for the winter. The years that intervened between the company's loss of the Blackfriars at the end of 1596 and their eventual reacquisition in 1608 had seen the building of the Globe, and the success of its first ten years. That success must have led them to revise Burbage's plan and to decide to keep the amphitheatre. What they instituted when playing reopened after the plague closure in 1609 was a more substantial version of what they had enjoyed before the city inns were closed to them, playing outdoors through the summer and indoors inside the city through the winter.

c. Playhouses Built for the Players

The new playhouses of 1599 and 1600 that were built as part of the change of locations by the Lord Chamberlain's and Lord Admiral's Men set the standard for playing in London. Both playhouses were built with Privy Council authority. They were designed for companies which had used their predecessors for the past six years and knew what they wanted; one of them was even owned by the company itself. In their joint role as financier and impresario for their resident company

Edward Alleyn and his father-in-law Philip Henslowe paid for the building of the Fortune. Through what in the long run turned out to be a fortunate set of accidents its own players became the financiers and impresarios of the other playhouse. That is how Shakespeare as an actor and sharer in his company came to own 12.5 per cent of the Globe, and later a similar share in the Blackfriars.

The Globe and the Fortune were the first playhouses ever to be built in London with government authorization. They also had the country's best companies to play in them. The Globe especially became the first and almost the only playhouse ever to be built by the players themselves, for themselves. The Blackfriars had been built for them by their impresario. The Fortune was built after them by another impresario. In material and practical terms the company that paid for the Globe set the bench mark for London playing. Shakespeare's company did secure their long-lost indoor playhouse in the Blackfriars precinct eventually, in 1608, and they used it thereafter for a version of what they had wanted in the early 1590s. That was their second breakthrough, at a time when the company had the king for their patron. Royal patronage for the best of the London companies lasted for the next thirty-four years.

That royal privilege, first signalled in 1583 when Queen Elizabeth made herself patron of a company, enhanced in 1594 by the two Privy Councillors and fixed for the privileged companies in 1599, ebbed with the royal fortunes in the 1640s, and vanished off the shoreline altogether for the eighteen years up to 1660 while Britain had no king. The long-developing tradition of Shakespearian playing was broken in 1642, and since then 300 years of new traditions, especially in the technicalities of theatre design and stage presentation, have brought performances of Shakespeare a long way from their origins in daylight and bare platform stages.

d. The Two Kinds of Playhouse

The auditorium at the Globe (see Fig. 2) reflected the radical and distinct social rankings through the whole range of its society. Beggars might be among the spectators on their feet next to the platform, struggling against their neighbours' elbows to keep a good position for viewing the action. Parents might be there with children. John Taylor,

the 'water poet', in *The praise, antiquity, and commodity of beggery,
beggers and begging* (London, 1628), tells how, at the Bankside, 'have
I seene a beggar with his many | Come in at a Play-house, all in for
one penny'. In bad weather the groundlings might choose to sit in
the lowest of the three ranks of galleries. The most privileged sat in the
galleries closest to the stage and above it, on the cushions that were
provided for the most costly benches in the 'gentlemen's rooms' or the
'lords' rooms'. In either of these literally elevated positions, they could
see the stage without having to look over the heads of the crowd who
stood in the yard. The lowest gallery in the circuit of three levels was
closest to the yard, and was where groundlings who could afford it
retreated when it rained. It was the least advantageous of the three
levels, since it not only meant watching the action from behind the
groundlings but had the worst acoustics of the three levels, behind
the shuffling groundlings and lacking the elevation of the two upper
galleries. Access to the lowest gallery was through the yard, whereas
the upper levels gained entry from the stair towers at the back. The
difference in the means of access helped to create a social distinction
between the lowest members of the audience, those either standing or
sitting nearest to the ground, and the folk in the upper levels in the
more steeply raked 'degrees'.

Each position in the auditorium reflected social status as well as
price with some precision. Each member of the Tudor public knew his
or her social place, and each place matched the social elevation, or at
least the social pretensions, of its occupant. The highest social ranks,
the nobles and gentry and their ladies, sat above and around the stage
platform. The 'middle region'[8] of audience in the thirty bays of the
upper galleries (fifteen bays on each of the upper two levels separated
by the framing timbers, each level jutting forward over the one
beneath), was occupied by gentry and the richer citizens. Access to
the upper levels was by the stair turrets at the back of the galleries. For
the lowest gallery access was through the yard, by an '*ingressus*' as
shown in the Swan drawing (see Fig. 1). If it rained, people who had
chosen to stand in the yard could move to shelter and a seat by paying a
second penny which let them retreat into the lowest gallery via the
'*ingressus*'.

In effect, the lower you were in the open-air playhouse the lower
your social status. Artisans and craftsmen, apprentices, house servants

and those of the unemployed who could afford it crammed into the yard, the rough-surfaced floor on which the stage platform stood, inside the polygonal circuit of bays. For their minimal price of admission these customers had nothing to sit on, and no roof over their heads. They were even closer to the stage than the nobles, but they saw the action from below instead of from above. The most expensive places gave an unmatched view of the whole action on the stage, although an on-stage duel when seen from the level of the combatants' feet by those standing alongside the stage in the yard had its own special pleasures.

The precision of this social positioning in the auditorium was matched in life by a complex set of signals, a familiar pattern or 'decorum' of how to behave so as to acknowledge the status of the people you met. Clothing signified social rank, and the body language that went with each rank was second nature to anyone living in Tudor society. Many of these decorums were exercised routinely in the body signals the players used. Without recognizing these stock actions, we miss features that would have clarified many aspects of the play, from the identification of status to character and attitude at any given moment. Not to obey the standard patterns of familiar social behaviour was a deliberate act, an active breach of decorum that spoke eloquently about a character's attitude, especially his opinion of those he was speaking to. Because cultural practices have shifted we have lost any idea of such eloquent body language. Hamlet's own status, for instance, and the different attitudes he adopted for everyone he spoke to, were eloquent features of the original staging.

The yard offered the minimal status, ground level, and only the lowest socially stood there. Everyone else could literally rise above them even when sitting in the lowest rank of the galleries. Hamlet himself invented the word 'groundlings' to describe these understanders. A groundling was a loach, a small ground-feeding freshwater fish, its mouth a huge sucker for feeding off the stones on a river bottom. The *Oxford English Dictionary* attributes the first use of this word, meaning a loach or small ground-feeding fish, to Philemon Holland's translation of Pliny, published in 1601, the year that *Hamlet* first appeared. These small fish with big mouths looking up at the players on stage were also called ignorant gapers, a term Jonson used in his attack on the 'scenicall strutting and furious vociferation' of the earlier age (*Works*, viii. 587). The more sarcastic playwrights called them 'under-standing men'. The groundlings did have some comforts. The yard surface was made of compacted ash, mixed in with a proportion of hard nutshells and similar debris (probably a by-product of the local soap factories, which smashed and boiled hazelnuts to make the lye for their soap, while the fires for the boiling created large amounts of ash and clinker).[9] This surface was porous enough to let the rain soak through, so that feet might be kept fairly dry, and yet it compacted down hard enough not to generate too much noise from the shuffling of restless feet.

The need for daylight to perform in left the amphitheatres vulnerable to the onset of bad weather, but less intrusively than we might think. For all the huge quantity of audience they could pack in, the open-air venues were intimate in the proximity they afforded to the stage. It was the weather which was the outsider at performances. In any case, playgoers in the galleries and boxes were well protected from rain, and most of them from the sun too. The topmost ring of galleries was thatched, and each level jutted out over the level below, in the standard mode of Tudor timber construction, designed to protect walls from rain seepage. Playgoers in the yard could get some protection from rain by standing well back against the lowest level, under the jutting galleries and thatch. Three feet in from the lowest bays, however, was not a good position during and after rain. The drips from a line of thatch that is nearly forty feet above your head can be painful, as well as wetting. The woollen 'flat caps' which artisans and apprentices wore had their uses in the yard.

Like the galleries, the stage platform was covered from rain and sun. Its roof was a large canopy that stretched over the stage out from the top gallery wall into the middle of the yard. This canopy or 'heavens' was a wooden roof covering the full extent of the platform. It projected out over the stage from a height similar to that of the top level of the galleries. The undersurface of the 'heavens' was painted colourfully with designs indicating its function as sky. The hut above it housed descent machinery, and boys dressed as gods or goddesses could be lowered from it to the stage. A boy played the goddess Juno in *The Tempest*'s masque, and seems to have been slowly lowered to stage level, where he/she was welcomed by the other boy goddesses. In *Cymbeline* the god Jupiter floated below the heavens on an eagle, throwing fireworks to simulate thunderbolts. As king of the gods, he may have been played by an adult player.

Apart from the features set in the *frons scenae*, the wall backing the stage and providing the entrance-ways for the players, the only distinctive feature the stage platform had was the two round wooden pillars painted to look like Roman columns of marble. The stage pillars were the single most conspicuous and ornate feature of the stage to register with Johannes De Witt on his visit to the Swan in 1596. They were there to support the canopy of the heavens, rising on each side of the stage some way in from the sides and front. Their weighty presence, the double pillars of the world, was the only major feature on the stage itself. At almost 1,200 square feet in size, the stage platform was a wide open space and except for the two pillars and the colourfully-carved and painted *frons* with its broad tapestry and its openings the main feature was its emptiness. In such a plain space movement was expansive. The only means of concealment for hiding or eavesdropping entailed standing behind one of the posts, where a player concealing himself would always be clearly visible to at least two-thirds of the surrounding audience. Such concealment was as implausible a deception as all the rest of the acting game. The groundlings surrounding the stage had to piece out the imperfections of these daylight games of 'play' in the energy of their imaginations.

The disposition of audience in these open-air playhouses reflected the origins of playing in the marketplaces of country towns, and its focus on the commoners who would throng in the town square. The higher social levels were almost an afterthought, an extension of the basic provision, carefully located close to the stage and literally elevated above the common throng, but less positive and less directly involved as a result of their placing in the actual business of sharing the experience of the play. Their location surrounding the stage made the groundlings much the most active participants in the game of playing. It was this demotic and populist sharing that the indoor playhouses abandoned.

In the earlier years, so far as staging and acting were concerned, the indoor venues differed from the open playhouses only in the priority they gave to the rich and their exclusion of groundlings. At the Blackfriars and later at the Cockpit and Salisbury Court halls players who were trained in the open-air venues performed the same plays in the same ways they were used to at the outdoor venues. Change came about because of the differences in the auditoria rather than in the plays or the players. Audiences were more comfortable, quieter, and more passive. They were indoors, in a candle-lit hall, enjoying pauses with music between each act of the play, and a more settled atmosphere instead of the non-stop gallop of an outdoor play. The indoor venues were not congenial to the use of fireworks attached to stage devils, nor the loud musical instruments and swords clashing on shields used in battle scenes. The famous Blackfriars consort of musicians, playing stringed and woodwind instruments in the music room, quite literally set a quieter tone for the occasion than the off-stage noises familiar at the outdoor venues.

Seated audiences also exchange less energy with the players than crowds standing around the stage, and the players reduced their voice levels and probably their physical gestures accordingly. The smaller stage space and its restrictions on stage movement led to the writing of plays featuring wit-combats and verbal interplay rather than swordplay. Prescient Shakespeare wrote only one of his plays, *The Tempest*, for staging at the Blackfriars.[10] Its off-stage music, its songs, its two spectacles (a banquet visited by a harpy, and a masque), its lack of fights or fireworks, the large proportion of scenes that call for few players on stage, in later years all became standard features of the plays written for the indoor venues. Only its opening storm scene called for loud noise and a scramble of most of the company's players over the stage. This was conceivably designed as a surprise for the seated gallants who had been lulled into the expectation of social harmony by the preliminary concert of the Blackfriars ensemble in the music room from which the ship's captain now roared and whistled his hectic orders to the boatswain on stage.

This account will focus chiefly on the outdoor staging practices. They were the venues for which the original traditions developed and were fixed by 'the glory of the banke', as Jonson called the Globe in his 'Execration upon Vulcan' (*Works*, viii. 209), and by its chief scriptwriter. Most of the traditions worked equally in all playing practices. In both kinds of playhouse, whether lit by sun or candlelight, the audiences were always visible. This helped to make metatheatricality, a self-conscious awareness that the stage could only present illusions, a much more prominent feature of the staging than the new forms of cinematic realism generally give us today. The suspension of disbelief had to be willing, and the writers and players often insisted on making it quite explicit.

e. The Staging Traditions

Staging plays that had to be portable was a tradition intensified by the practice of mounting a new play at the suburban playhouses every day. There is no record of any company staging any of its plays for more than one day at a time until July 1613, when the Globe was burned down on the third performance of a new play, *Henry VIII, or All Is True.* Even when travelling ceased to be the norm for the major London companies, the forms of staging reflected that constant turnover of plays. Performances had none of the leisure and intensity that attend modern staging, and the players always had to rely on their experience when confronted with a new challenge.

Each company worked as a team. The standard shape for a company started with eight or ten 'sharers', a core of experienced players who took most of the speaking parts, and who had equal shares in both the income and the expenditure of their company. Some of the players took young boys under their wing in imitation of the system that every town guild operated for training apprentices in their trades. So long as the boys were young enough to have unbroken voices (real apprentices signed on at 17, by when their voices would have broken) they played the women's parts. When their voices broke, if they had proved themselves capable they might stay on to play juvenile leads, eventually buying themselves a 'share' in the company's fortunes. Most companies had a senior player who took the chief decisions about where to travel to and which plays to perform. Finances were generally controlled by two of the senior sharers. In later years the companies based in London might break up a 'share' into fractions, so that an ambitious hireling might begin buying his way in with a half or quarter-share. But the democratic or teamwork principle of 'sharing' remained the basis of company organization throughout.

For its time it was an exceptional mixture of entrepreneurial adventure and collective responsibility. Since the company's good fortune depended absolutely on every sharer literally playing his part

in every day's work, the sharer system demanded professional commitment and complete interdependency. Every play required a similar
number of players to take part, and every player had to be perfect in
his 'part' for each day's choice of play. Every player had his own
particular aptitude. He might develop a specific 'line', and get the
parts set for the heroic soldier, or the dignified king, the romantic lead,
the 'senex' or comic old man, or the clown. That made casting a new
play fairly straightforward, but if one of the sharers fell ill it could
make problems. The chances that ten or more men working and living
closely together while they travelled the Tudor countryside could
all remain permanently fit for their work are minimal. High-speed
adjustments to the casting schedules must have been normal practice.
When Edward Alleyn, leading Strange's Men on tour in 1593 fell ill
at Bath, the company had to transfer his famous parts to another
sharer.[11]

Such a system of rapid production by teamwork imposed traditional
rule-of-thumb staging practices onto every performance. Playing in
London gave the companies greater resources in theatre venues and in
spare players, but it laid a heavy load on the creation of new plays, and
rules of thumb must have determined every detail, from swordfights
and processional entrances and exits to noises 'within'. While in the
country three or four plays was an ample number to travel with, in
London the companies that played at the Rose through the 1590s had
to have more than thirty ready to stage each year.

In London from the time the company bought a writer's playscript
the new play had barely three weeks to be brought to performance. In
that brief period it went through the book-keeper's preparation of the
playbook and a 'plot' was made for the staging. This work included the
identification of what properties were needed and when in the script,
checking that the doubling of parts did not make it impossible for one
player to reappear in a fresh costume at the right moment, and not
least obtaining any special costumes and props. Ordinary costumes
were the concern of individual players, but the company had to supply
everything out of the ordinary. The same three weeks called for scribes
to copy each of the 'parts' or major speaking roles and for the players to
learn them (the longest parts might comprise eight hundred or more
lines of verse), before the play could be blocked for stage movement
and all entrances and exits and properties checked through a morning

or two's rehearsal. It was a factory production line, yet each end-product was an individual work.

The chief difference between Shakespearian and modern acting is perhaps indicated more clearly than in anything else by the fact that an Alleyn or Burbage had to be able to deliver more than four thousand lines of verse in six different plays through every week of his life while he worked in London. Tours with no more than three or four plays must have felt like a holiday in comparison. No modern actor would dream of trying to work at that rate. In a lifelong system whose teamwork laid relentless demands on every member of the team, it seems almost unimaginably challenging. It is not surprising that some of the leading players such as Martin Slater and Thomas Swinnerton seem to have avoided playing in London. Slater, who took a company to Edinburgh in 1599 to play before King James, spent all of his working life travelling outside London with companies which staged a strictly limited number of plays. He chose that course despite having a large family in London (in 1609 he is recorded as having a wife and nine other dependants there).[12]

The effect this high-speed delivery of a hugely demanding repertory had on the staging of the plays, when the venues themselves were so uncertain and variable, is difficult to comprehend while our under-standing of the standard practices the players used in their system is still so minimal. The early players learned their lines from handwritten 'parts' that gave them only the preceding line or half-line as their cue to speak each speech. They worked alone on how to deliver their speeches and how to 'personate' their roles. They may have developed standard gestures to express specific emotions, most of which are still recognizable. Putting the hand over the heart as a show of intense feeling, pressing the brow with the back of the hand for worry, wring-ing the hands in guilt or repentance were all recognized forms recorded in the occasional instruction book about oratory or depicted as visible expressions for the deaf. Weeping and laughing, or specific gestures like concealing one's expression by pulling the brim of the hat down over one's face are called for in various playscripts. In *Love's Labours Lost*, 3.1.13–16 the boy Mote tells Don Armado about a lover's body language: 'your hat penthouse-like o'er the shop of your eyes, with your arms crossed on your thin-belly doublet like a rabbit on a spit, or your hands in your pocket like a man after the old painting'.

Both players and their audiences must have developed a large reper-
toire of gestural expressions of this kind.

The companies, having so little time for rehearsal, must have
blocked their crowd scenes in standard forms familiar to every player.
Those few scripts which show signs of having been used by a book-
keeper for prompting purposes indicate that a great deal was left to the
players themselves. Printed texts of plays used as playbooks, such as the
Folger Library's copy of *The Merry Milkmaids*, staged at the Red Bull
in 1619,[13] suggest that the chief duty of the book-keeper during a
performance was to alert each of the players for their next entrance
roughly nine lines in advance, to have the necessary props ready for
use, and to prompt any off-stage noises at the right moment. Once a
player was on stage his conduct of his scene was his own affair. The
surviving copy of the 'booke' of *The Merry Milkmaids* indicates that
once he had them on stage the book-keeper was never concerned
about how to get them off again. That was their business. The tradition that developed with proscenium-arch theatres of using a prompter sitting just off-stage at one side to prompt the actors who forgot
their lines would not work on the early stages. Behind a large platform
like the Globe's with its strong *frons scenae* built out of oak and lime
plaster, it is not easy to hear much of the dialogue on stage. The
flanking stage doors behind which the players had to stand while
waiting to hear their cues to enter had to stand slightly ajar if the cue
was to be heard. Conceivably the occasional references in stage directions to knocking at the door may be misleading, and the stage
entrances were all really done through hangings that fronted all of
the doorways. More likely, though equally conjectural, is the possibility that whenever kings or nobles were on stage an attendant would
stand beside the door ready to open it when his master prepared to
leave. All great houses and palaces were peopled with house servants in
livery standing ready to do such services, and it would be normal for
the theatres to reflect the same custom.

Chapters 4–6 of this book confront the question of how they made
their entrances and exits on stage, as a specific but pervasive instance of
early staging. Such basic questions are a fundamental element in the
attempt to identify the standard procedures for performing into which
this rich resource of plays was originally set.

f. The Plays and the Conditions of Performance

The texts of the plays that have survived from this extraordinary period are far from being the immaculate record of the author's intentions that most editions of the plays aim to provide. They are by far the most substantial record of what was performed, but they started only as raw scripts, the words the players had to learn. The original manuscripts did represent the writer's concept of the play as he wanted it to be staged, but the production system changed the original concepts radically as the play moved from author's idea towards what the players finally put on the stage. As Peter Blayney describes it in his introduction to the second Norton facsimile of the First Folio, 'the author's final draft is essentially only the raw material for perform-ance'.[14] In this lengthy and fluid collaborative process, there was no single fixed moment when a written script, an authoritative record of the 'performance text' could ever be identified. No such thing as a 'prompt book' emerged, in the form of the script agreed for staging by the company. As we have seen, there was no regular prompter, since the strong physical structure of the oak-made *frons scenae* which provided the entry-points for the open stages of the first playhouses made it difficult for anyone behind it to hear what was being said on stage. Nor was there a regular script, since every performance might cut or trim the script which the Master of the Revels had officially approved. Each company had a book-keeper, who served as stage manager and holder of the manuscript from which each player's speak-ing part was copied. He marked his manuscript to prepare each player's entry and to note the props that might be needed for each scene, but once a player was out on the stage what followed was his own affair. A forgetful player might get some help from his fellows if he forgot his lines, but the book-keeper left him to his own devices, not even noting when or how he should make his exit. The most frequent occasion when the full text with the Master's signature was cut was whenever a player forgot his lines.

A fixed script or edition of any Shakespeare or Renaissance play, the printed form in which we customarily receive our versions of that peculiarly brilliant body of drama, is a chimera. Modern editions are made out of the varying fragments of record that have survived about the texts, shaped by a lot of editorial assumptions rooted in precedents from other texts. They aim to reproduce the one unique and ideal text which the original players always tried to enact on stage. In practice, no matter what the original author wanted and prescribed in the manuscript which he sold the company, or what the Revels Office authorized to be spoken, a company would perform whatever their immediate circumstances dictated. Companies altered their perform- ances day by day, changing the staging according to which kinds of resource that day's venue provided, which actor was sick and had to be replaced, or which piece of stage action a player might decide could be improved. Cutting the script, either to fit the limited time available for a performance, or to eliminate sections of the script that had not worked well in the previous performance, or to censor dubious pieces of dialogue which might give offence or which had become irrelevant, was a standard practice.

g. Stage Directions as Records

In the printed texts which are the most tangible record of the original performances, stage directions were mostly standardized into a kind of shorthand, although whether they were designed for the use of players or readers in the source for any particular text is often unclear. Almost all of the six hundred or so plays that have survived between the time when Shakespeare started writing for the stage and the closure of the theatres in 1642 exist only in print. Printed versions were made to be sold to readers, but the manuscripts from which these texts were printed often came from the companies that performed them.

It has long been assumed that the company playbook served as the authoritative version of the play, the prompt book used to correct the players when their memory slipped. Some authoritative manuscripts clearly did exist up to 1642, but how many of them were transferred into print unchanged, and at what step in the long process of transfer from author to stage is not easy to establish. There have been more questions than answers over the problem about how much editorial revision was introduced between the manuscript playbooks and the printed versions. The source manuscripts for Shakespeare's own plays have been identified as existing in a wide variety of forms. They run from the manuscript or 'foul papers' that the author first delivered to the company, to a copy of the company's own playbook as modified in performance and used in the playhouse to correct an existing quarto of the play in print, down to defective copies assembled by a group of dissident players who wrote out their lines from their memories of the original performances. None of them is likely to have been the ideal text dignified by the Master of the Revels's signature. That was far too precious a company asset to be released into the grubby hands of a printer, unless the company 'broke', and the survivors had no other company to take them to. Each kind of manuscript source has its own deficiencies.

h. The Evidence of the Play-Texts

Besides all the textual variants which this variety of versions evoked, each form of transmission would generate a slightly different kind of stage direction. Standard terms such as 'enter', 'exit', 'manet', 'within', 'above', and 'discovered' were the familiar vocabulary of staging, and normally meant the same thing to everyone, whatever kind of manuscript the play was printed from. Special staging or effects were more variable. Some of the stage directions in *The Tempest*, for instance, especially the one which specifies that '*with a quaint device the banquet vanishes*', seem to have been set down with a reader in mind. Such a direction would hardly have been a help to the players working out how to stage the scene. In general, Shakespeare's own stage directions were regrettably minimal. His cryptic instructions about the monument scene in *Antony and Cleopatra* have led critics and directors to build mountains of speculation without any clear conclusion about what Shakespeare wanted. Possibly Shakespeare was cryptic because he expected to be on hand at rehearsals to explain his intentions, although Thomas Heywood, the nearest equivalent to Shakespeare in his work as an actor and playwright contracted to a specific playing company, was usually far more explicit in writing out his directions. He was also a lot more demanding over staging than Shakespeare, whose tightfistedness in his personal finances may also be reflected in the economy of the demands he laid on his company for staging his plays.

There are a few changes visible over the years in authorial practices for writing stage directions. Through the late 1580s and the beginning of the 1590s when the playing companies first began to make regular use of the amphitheatres in London's suburbs there are signs that the writers' ambitions were growing. They were beginning to realize the possibilities the new amphitheatres could offer. Robert Greene signalled his vision some time before his death in 1592 in composing *Alphonsus of Aragon*, when he gave Venus her final exit either on foot or '*if you can conveniently, let a chaire come downe from the top of the stage, and draw her up*'.[15] Several authors wrote hopeful directions like this through the period up to 1594. Fresh ambition of this kind in writing for the London amphitheatres may help to explain why Shakespeare's own early plays are so much more demanding than those he wrote later. Two in particular, *Titus Andronicus* and *Romeo and Juliet*, lay down some distinctly heavier demands for their staging than any he wrote later.[16] Both plays demand the maximum number of the fixed resources the open-air stages had: a stage trap, a balcony space capable of holding several players, underneath it an opening wide enough to allow a bed to be thrust out onto the stage, and two entry doors on the flanks of the stage. The flanking entry doors were standard, but none of Shakespeare's later plays call for all of these features, and no venue outside London could have supplied them. More than half of the later plays do not even ask for an 'above' and a balcony scene. After 1594, when the plays were being written for staging at the Rose and the Theatre and their successors, Shakespeare's demands over what his venues could supply him with shrank. Why that should be we can only guess. The plays other authors wrote for the Rose and the Fortune laid down even heavier demands. Conceivably Shakespeare kept his mind on the limitations of the venues available when the company went on its travels. He did not expand his requirements until the last years, when he asked for Cleopatra's monument, Jupiter in *Cymbeline* throwing fireworks while mounted on his flying eagle, Hermione's concealment behind the hangings as a statue on a plinth in *The Winter's Tale*, and the vanishing banquet and the masque with Juno descending in *The Tempest*.

The possible shifts in Shakespeare's own ideas about staging before and after 1594, and in his last plays, pose the danger of influencing thinking about the original staging more than they should. How much the traditions changed, for the writers who conceived the plays and the companies that brought them to performance, it is not easy to say.

Certainly with such an intense and rapidly developing repertory we might expect the fashions in plays and hence in their staging to go on developing year by year. Other writers made much more extravagant demands of their employers, and some companies seem to have made strenuous efforts to meet the demands. Some changes in the nature of the plays are evident, but the only general changes in staging practices for which there is much evidence are first, the beginning of longer runs in the second decade of the seventeenth century—*Henry VIII* was on its third afternoon of performance when its cannon set the Globe's thatch on fire—and secondly a narrowing in the variety of play staged at particular playhouses. Once companies of adult players started using indoor playhouses, the repertories diverged. They took on the more innovatory plays, while the amphitheatres kept the older plays. *Faustus, Tamburlaine,* and *The Spanish Tragedy* were still running at the Fortune and the Red Bull into the 1640s, when they were known as 'citizen' playhouses, catering to more working-class and conservative tastes.

These shifts all affect the forms and the varieties of staging that might be identified for the plays of this period. The fragmentary evidence for the original staging needs to be read carefully. Each fragment was influenced by the period of development in which the play was written, the design of the playhouse for which it was written, and the particular kind of audience expectation prevailing at that type of playhouse.

In this kind of study there are many areas of uncertainty, and a related danger that too much weight can be put on individual instances as a mark of general practice. Might not a stage direction written to explain the staging for a specific scene have been written out so explicitly not because it was standard but precisely because it was not to be done in the normal way? Beyond the more practical features of staging lie other obscurities, all the patterns of Elizabethan behaviour as players reproduced them on stage. The traditions of playing entailed styles and nuances of style that we have lost. We can identify many symbols, such as women's wigs when worn loose signifying madness, and many games with cross-dressing which exploited the fact that women's roles were played by boys. The dream of rediscovering an 'authentic' original performance is of course a chimera, for the originals varied from day to day and in the minds of individual playgoers.

It is possible, however, to sharpen our sense of what the plays were designed to do, and in the process learn a little more about the elements where we tend to lay an unthinkingly modern gloss over the bare original.

i. The Play as Performance Text

Let us take, as a particularly revealing instance, one example of a few of the things that might be learned from studying *Hamlet* as a performance text and trying to reconstruct how it was originally meant to be performed. It is an example which can augment the critical process which has related the ghost to all of the four figures in the play who are set in parallel to one another as children of murdered parents: Hamlet himself, Laertes, Fortinbras, and Ophelia. Of the four children, Hamlet is matched on the revenger side by Laertes and Fortinbras. One attempts to take ruthless revenge for his father's murder and dies for it, the other holds back from revenge and so proves to be the only survivor, taking everything as his 'fortune'. Ophelia, also faced with a father murdered, takes the alternative option canvassed by Hamlet in his 'To be or not to be' soliloquy, the bare bodkin, by going mad and committing suicide. These three alternatives to Hamlet, one a suicide victim and the other two revenger figures, cast lights of different hues on his own options and his resolution of them.

These parallels have a strong bearing on a question that underlies much of the play, the ethics of revenge. The 'wild justice' of revenge, as Bacon called it, was condemned in Shakespeare's time as anti-Christian. Elizabethans read the Book of Genesis as saying that such justice was for God alone to impose. Vengeance is *mine*, said the Lord, over Cain's killing of Abel, *I* will repay. Shakespeare had already played an elaborate game with that injunction in the opening scene of *Richard II*, when Bullingbrook invoked Cain in demanding the right to avenge the murder of his uncle. In the play which was in *Hamlet*'s time the archetype for all revenge plays, Thomas Kyd's *The Spanish Tragedy*, Hieronymo has a scene weighing the injunctions of the Bible against those of Seneca, who upheld revenge. He opts in favour of Seneca, with effects that are fatal to himself as revenger. His option is to accept damnation as the just reward for his successful revenge. Something like that stands behind Hamlet's long debate with himself, and his weighing of the options in the 'To be' soliloquy. The original staging underlined firmly all of these elements in the play.

Some of that can be seen in another feature of *The Spanish Tragedy* renewed in *Hamlet*. Shakespeare's text introduced changes to the revenge archetype, and the original audiences would have recognized those changes more easily than we can. Chief among them is the number of appearances of the ghost as the advocate of revenge. In Kyd's play the ghost of Don Andrea is personified as the initiator and observer of all the actions of the play. He returns as the play ends to gloat over the success of the policy of revenge. Hamlet's dead father, on the other hand, does not return at the end of the play. Instead he appears in the form of a surrogate presence which would have been recognized in its visual features in the original staging, but of which we are deprived by our blind reading of the words. He returned in a distinctive shape which has some striking implications for our reading of the play.

When the ghost first appeared in the original staging he climbed out of the trapdoor in the middle of the Globe's stage. The understage area had a symbolic function as hell, the place into which Faustus and Barabbas are cast. It was opposed to the 'heavens' over the stage from which gods were occasionally lowered. The earth was the stage platform in between. *Hamlet*'s ghost rose from hell, dressed in full armour with his field-marshal's truncheon, to warn the sentinels, and then to summon Hamlet with the news of his duty to take revenge. By contrast with this emphasis on his purgatorial residence, for his mid-play appearance he appeared through the central opening, the 'Portal',[17] wearing his nightgown and nightcap in Gertrude's closet and stepping obliviously over Polonius, who lay sprawled by the arras where Hamlet killed him. With that act Hamlet has become a murderer, and so the potential victim of the other children of a murdered father, Laertes and Ophelia. By then we know that Hamlet has chosen to take revenge, and we might, if we choose, recognize his murder of Polonius as the clinching mark of his eventual damnation.

Other events intervene before the revenges bring more deaths, though. First we see Fortinbras for the first time. He, the revenger of his father's death who has been diverted from his revenge, appears on stage as his army's general dressed exactly like the dead King Hamlet in his appearance in Act I, in armour and carrying a general's truncheon. Fortinbras wears the ghost's military gear, in contrast to Hamlet, who is still dressed like a student for his trip to England. Fortinbras in armour is a surrogate for the ghost of King Hamlet. And then there is the great trapdoor scene, where all the associations of revenge and damnation come together. The trapdoor initially serves as Ophelia's grave, with the gravedigger quibbling over whether she should be damned for killing herself. That resonance enhances the idea of the grave-trap as the gateway to hell. Later Laertes jumps down into the trap with her, an acknowledgement of the damnation which his own revenge role will bring him. And Hamlet, making one of his characteristically oblique associations between his memory of the trap as the ghost's point of entry and of revenge as leading to hell, cries out that he is his father's ghost ('This is I, *Hamlet* the Dane') and leaps in after Laertes.

The original audiences saw that as a union of the three children of murdered fathers joined symbolically in hell. Such a neat conjunction of the iconic point of this stage feature uniting three candidates for revenge set the fourth revenge figure, Fortinbras, apart from the others. He is the only one whose father died in battle, not as a murder victim. He is the only one who forsakes revenge. He never approaches the trapdoor to hell. And he is the one who returns after all the deaths, still dressed like the ghost, to claim his good fortune by taking over the crown of Denmark.

The role of Fortinbras in the play's conclusion is a deeply complex one. How you read it depends on what you make of the symbols that surround it, and the one non-standard thing that he chooses to do. Finding a group of corpses at the Danish court, including the king and queen as well as young Laertes and Hamlet, he picks out Hamlet as the one figure amongst them all who, he concludes, deserves a soldier's funeral. He ignores all the others, most remarkably the king whose crown he has just claimed. Horatio has not yet told him anything of the complex story, nor who is its hero and who its villain. So why does he choose Hamlet for the soldier's funeral?

Part of the answer to that might be found in his appearance as a surrogate for the ghost of the dead King Hamlet. He fulfils the revenge tradition laid down with *The Spanish Tragedy* by appearing as a version of the gloating ghost, celebrating the success of the earthly revenger he had appointed at the play's outset. 'Bear Hamlet like a soldier to the stage', he orders, as if he thought Hamlet had the potential to be a match for the soldier Fortinbras and the dead soldier-king. That thought he immediately discredits in the bland and obtuse assumption he voices next, that Hamlet had never been 'put on'. Perhaps he is showing how little Hamlet's own highly complex reading of the revenge task was capable of being understood, in a world where Hamlet's militant father certainly had no sense of the burden he laid on his studious son, and where a man who appears in the shape of a surrogate for the militant and mindless King Hamlet will succeed by 'fortune' to the throne of Denmark.

By far the best way to show how a performance in the original conditions might have been experienced is to describe the staging of a particular play at the Globe. The final chapter of this book tries to do that by giving an account of how *Hamlet* might have been staged at the original Globe. We have chosen *Hamlet* for this purpose partly because so many versions of the play in modern performance styles are available today, and partly because it exemplifies so many distinctive features of the original staging at the Globe. We even know that Richard Burbage played the first Hamlet, and what he looked like. The only deficiency of *Hamlet* for use as an exemplar of early staging is its failure to make any use of the stage balcony, the 'above'. There are Shakespearian reasons for that—its focus is on the earth, and on hell beneath the earth, not upwards towards heaven. Everyone in the play, even Ophelia, is in the end disqualified from a place in heaven. Only the stage 'heavens' are present to gesture at, as a remote observer of the earthly events. It is a play about the ungodliness of revenge. As such, the way it emphasizes the trapdoor and understage area rather than the stage balcony and the 'heavens' above might be seen as a tacit emblem of its theology.

Such complexities, however, should be held back until we come to the conclusion of this study of the multitude of revealing details in the evidence for the early staging practices. Many other devices that the players used need to be looked at before we can come to any sort of conclusion about how Shakespeare conceived his plays in performance. For instance we need to find a means to explain the thoroughly enigmatic and unrevealing use of the bald terms '*Enter*' and '*Exit*'. When written for stages which normally had as many as three possible places for the players to enter and leave by, those terms are distinctly unhelpful. The next chapter will look at the material aids the Tudors had for their staging, and the three subsequent chapters will examine the procedures that controlled movement on and off and around the early stages. Studied systematically, this work reveals unpredictable features of the ways bodies were expected to move on the early stages, and the shorthand ways of marking such moves in the surviving texts. Chapter 7 will then offer an account of *Hamlet*'s staging, in the light of the evidence offered in the first six chapters.

Other Aspects of
Shakespearian Staging

a. Symbolic Staging: Costumes and Properties

Everything used to dress and equip the players on the early stages was symbolic. Because resources at the early venues were unpredictable, all the staging had to be flexible and all the properties had to be portable. Every object and item of clothing worked as a signifier. A cloak signified an outdoor location, riding boots indicated a traveller, a night-cap showed someone roused from his bed. Special signifiers augmented the routine signs. A sword in its scabbard made a gentleman, velvet cloth a lady, gold lace a nobleman or woman. A ghost wore a recognizable shroud, 'antics' or clowns wore their own distinctly incongruous and old-fashioned suits, Hamlet's funeral black, Malvolio's yellow stockings, a lover demonstrating his melancholy by sighing and pulling the brim of his hat down over his face, all these were instant signifiers of mood and plan.

Dress signified social status, and for the players it signified with equal weight their professional habit of disguising and 'counterfeiting'. Robes and furred gowns hid the low status of the player beneath. But it was more than a simple matter of dressing up beyond one's status. The deception of playing was very largely a matter of dress, and of audiences accepting appearances as, however transient, the theatrical reality. In *Twelfth Night* Viola and Sebastian were made into identical twins not by their faces but by their similar dress. In 4.4 of *The Taming of the Shrew* the Pedant when disguised as Vincentio simply wears a different hat to confirm which role he is assuming. The changing dress of the victimized characters in *King Lear*, from Lear himself to Edgar as Poor Tom, showed how their status shrank. Lear starts with his crown and regalia, reappears in more casual clothes as a huntsman, loses even that when he rages bareheaded in the storm, and finally stands crowned with flowers as a mad parody of his original kingly status. Edgar moves from noble dress to the material deprivation of nakedness under a blanket. Reality was what clothes disguised. As Ben Jonson complained in his 'Expostulation with Inigo Jones',[1] 'No velvet sheath you wear, will alter kind.' Clothes only made the appearance of the man, and the metatheatrical nature of the experience required the faithful willingly to suspend their disbelief in what they saw worn on the outside, and to take it as the play's reality.

Thanks to the Henslowe and Alleyn papers, we have lists of the stock of costumes kept by the Admiral's Men who played at the Rose and the Fortune amphitheatres. For ordinary parts, when hired men played household servants or messengers, ordinary street wear was sufficient, and the players used their own clothes. The company built up its resources of costume or 'apparel' only for parts with a social status well above the player range, such as nobles and rich gentry, or for special parts such as cardinals and monks, Robin Hood and Tamburlaine. Not many of them were made specially for any one role. Mostly these investments in apparent affluence were for general use, though there was quite a heavy investment in special attire. An inventory of the Admiral's Men from 1598 lists more than 300 costumes, less than one in ten identified by the specific character they were designed for. The special costumes included '6 green coats for Robin Hood' and Robin's hat, '1 green gown for Marion', four pairs of 'red strossers', or trousers, along with four janissaries' gowns for the Turkish characters in the various Rose plays that presented the wars round the Mediterranean, '4 torch-bearer's suits', '1 senator's gown, 1 hood, and 5 senator's capes', a ghost's suit and bodice, and a fool's coat, cap, and bauble, together with the rather enigmatic 'Eve's bodice', and in a later list of purchases '1 robe for to go invisible'.[2]

This was the main inventory of the Admiral's Men's properties, made by Henslowe in 1598 but now surviving only in a copy made by Edmond Malone in 1790. The three hundred items of apparel and over a hundred portable properties range from moss banks, two trees, one with golden apples and another for Tantalus, mattocks, a wooden leg, and the four 'Turk's heads' needed for a scene in *The Battle of Alcazar*, to 'ı tomb of Dido' and 'ı cauldron for the Jew' (in Marlowe's *Jew of Malta*).

As another category of playing assets, the inventory lists a total of twenty-nine playbooks in manuscript. Almost no playbooks of the period have survived. The more valuable the asset, the more likely it was to be worn out by heavy use. Eventually even paper will lose its essential value as a record of the spoken word. These playbooks, the manuscripts that had been read and 'allowed' by the Master of the Revels and which carried his signature on the last page to indicate his approval, were the single most valuable asset any playhouse or playing company possessed. What we prefer to call the 'playhouse manuscript', the licensed playbook, was the object that justified all the other properties a company owned. And it underwent heavy use. The company could not take a play into the country without carrying the licensed manuscript, because the Master's signature was their authority to perform it. The more popular the play, the more quickly the manuscript would erode. They would not readily release even the least popular of their play manuscripts to a printer, since it was unlikely to survive its stint of use by the compositors. Precious commodities though they were, it is not surprising that hardly any examples of these unique assets have survived.

Some of the items we might expect to find in a modern theatre's wardrobe are curiously absent from the Henslowe lists. The wigs that were needed for the boys to play women, for instance, get no mention. Nor do false beards. Perhaps, like ordinary clothing and properties like staves or cudgels, such items belonged to individual players, or, in the case of the women's wigs, to the boys' masters. Conceivably they were not valuable enough to be entered in the inventories. But equally absent is any indication that materials for facial make up of any kind were part of a company's resources. It does seem, from David Bradley's analysis of the plot and the most likely doubling pattern for *The Battle of Alcazar*,[3] that when they had to characterize a Moor, besides the wearing of turbans, long white gowns, and red trousers, they used either lampblack or coal to darken the face. In the *Masque of Blacknesse*, presented at Court in 1605, when Queen Anne and several of her ladies blacked up for the show, they even used tight headpieces of lawn appearing as closely curled black hair. Apart from the evidence for blacking up, though, there is little to suggest that using make up of any kind was a regular custom. Conceivably when Hermione returned in Act 5 of *The Winter's Tale* aged by sixteen years she wore a different wig with more grey in it. Leontes comments on her new wrinkles, but that may have been what Alan C. Dessen calls a 'fictional' statement rather than a 'theatrical' one, identifying a feature precisely because it is not there, and therefore needs to be specified in words if it is to be imagined.[4]

Another inventory of costumes, written in Edward Alleyn's hand in about 1602, shows what a wealth of colourful exhibitionism this aspect of early playing could give the players. It lists cloaks, doublets, and gowns made in fabrics that the Sumptuary laws reserved for the gentry: silks, satins, taffeta, and velvets. Some of these costumes were decorated with the gold or silver lace officially reserved for lords and ladies. The list of gowns includes 'a crimson robe striped with gold, faced with ermine', 'one wrought of cloth of gold', and 'one of red silk with gold buttons'. Doublets include 'a crimson satin case laced with gold lace all over', and 'black taffeta cut on black velvet laced with bugle'. Items such as 'spangled shoes' and a boy's costume in cloth of gold for general use were listed alongside 'Daniel's gown', 'Faustus's jerkin, his cloak', and 'Will Somers's coat'. This last appears in a list headed 'Antic suits', the comically old-fashioned costumes worn by the clowns who danced and sang the jigs.

Elizabethans loved colour. They painted their house interiors, they hung painted cloths on their walls if they could not afford tapestries, and above all everyone, playgoers or not, who could afford to, dressed as colourfully as they could. Faced with such competition and such an expectation, the players decorated their *frons scenae* with vividly colourful cloths and used their best attire to parade like mannequins. Tourists like Thomas Platter reported that the servants of noblemen would bring their masters' used costumes to sell to the players. Henslowe, and presumably the companies that he served as paymaster, invested as much in rich gowns as in playbooks.

But playbooks and attire were not the only resources the players needed. Musical instruments were another feature of the inventories. Henslowe's lists include three trumpets, a drum, a treble viol, a bass viol, a bandore, and a cittern. We know that some of the players, particularly those who played 'antic' parts, owned their own instruments. The 1605 will of Augustine Phillips, who played comic roles in the Shakespeare company, gave a gift of money along with two suits of clothes including a purple cloak, his sword and dagger, and a bass viol to his ex-apprentice boy. To his current apprentice he left money plus his cittern, bandore, and lute. He had evidently passed his own expertise with string instruments on to his pupils.

b. Portable Properties

The use of large properties was limited by the need to keep the plays portable. The court, to which selected companies were summoned each winter for the Christmas festivities, had the services of the Revels Office and its extensive stock of costumes and props to help them. On tour to Norwich or Coventry, though, when the total resources for transporting all the essentials, playbooks, costumes, musical instruments, properties, and company personnel were unlikely to be more than one cart and a few horses, nothing weighty would have been considered. The guildhalls could easily supply a magistrate's chair as a throne, since the meeting room in the guildhall where visiting companies performed for the mayor also served as the local court of justice. The need for the other major prop, a bed, was much less frequent, but local beds could be constructed or introduced if one was thought to be an essential feature. Little else was needed for most plays, even at home in London.

The largest and most weighty property to be used regularly was a throne. Thrones for judges to sit on when hearing legal cases, or the 'chair of state' on which the supreme judge, the king, sat, were major symbols of authority. Besides the gilded wooden chair on which the authority figure sat, they were backed by a 'cloth of estate', with the royal arms, and a small canopy overhead. This whole 'state' was positioned on a dais several steps high, so that the authority figure's head could be on a level with the person standing in front of him. As a regal throne, it was an essential feature of the trappings of kingship, like the crown and the orb and sceptre. On the stage it would have been located centrally, behind and between the stage pillars, but forward of the *frons scenae*. In the central 'deposition' scene of *Richard II*, 4.1, it serves as a character in the drama, standing empty while Bullingbrook and Richard argue in front of it, disputing whose right it is

to occupy it. Each stands with one hand clutching the crown, posses-
sion of which will entitle him to sit on the empty chair behind them.

The dais on which the chair of state stood may have had other uses
too. In *Julius Caesar*, 3.2, when Brutus enters for his oration to the
Romans, the stage direction reads '*Enter Brutus and goes into the Pulpit,
and Cassius, with the Plebeians.*' The fact that he is said to enter
followed by the others indicates that he does not speak from the upper
level, the stage balcony. Some object was available on the main stage. It
had to provide him with height, so that his head could be clearly visible
above the crowd. A dais could do that for him, elevating him as well as
it did the seated monarch. In the post-Catholic English churches of
the later sixteenth century the pulpit was replacing the altar as the
focus of worship. The analogy with the formal speeches delivered to
the Roman community first by Brutus and then by his rival Antony
would have been clear, but they did not need the material structure of a
church pulpit to represent it. It was certainly true that to put anything
resembling a real pulpit onto a stage in those times would have
brought major trouble down on the players.

In *Romeo and Juliet* a bed was an important accessory to the action.
In theory it marked first the marital union of the two lovers, which the
events transform until it became their pretended deathbed, before
their final union in a graveyard. In practice, we never see the pair in
bed together. The balcony and the trapdoor as grave serve for their
locations when they are together. Juliet's bed was used only for her
pretended death, alone. Elizabethan beds were normally wide enough
for two people side by side, and were always hung round with either
a vallance and hangings, as in four-poster beds, or a canopy hung
from the head end, to conceal the occupants. Stage beds were canopied, probably about four feet wide, an easy size to slide onto the stage
through the central opening, as called for by the many stage directions
demanding that a bed be 'put out'. Unlike *Romeo and Juliet* and
Cymbeline, where the married Imogen has to sleep alone because
her husband is in exile, the bed in Act 5 of *Othello* did serve for
the pair of married lovers. Desdemona would have been carried out
by two stage hands for her final scene in *Othello* on the canopied
bed which was to hold the bodies of the married couple, white
Desdemona allied inseparably with black Othello, in the play's final
tableau.

Beds were not used for the sick, unless the scene called for the literal presentation of a deathbed. Ailing characters sat in a sick chair, wrapped in a rug or kerchief. King Henry dying in the Jerusalem chamber at Westminster in *2 Henry IV* was probably laid out on his bed, but John of Gaunt when sick in *Richard II*, 2.1, sat in a special chair.[5] The dying Antony may have been bound into a similar chair in the later play, when Cleopatra had to haul him up to her monument. They were more readily portable than beds, and for any scene except the finale of a play it was always useful to have some means to carry dying people off-stage before they actually died. Getting rid of all the bodies after the finale of a tragedy is one of the more complex problems about the early staging. Many tragedies end with a funeral procession, which entailed carrying the bodies out through the central opening, but at the end of *Hamlet*, as described above, it is possible that the dead were expected to get up and make their bows, and walk off. The dead could not easily do that, however, in any scene before the finale.

The stage hangings were another much-used property, almost the only one that served as a fixed feature of the early stages. They alternated with the stage pillars as the chief place of concealment for spying scenes. In this role the pillars served mainly in comedies, for instance in the games played in *Much Ado About Nothing*, 2.3 and 3.1, on Benedick and Beatrice. The hangings tended to serve in more serious situations, most obviously for Claudius and Polonius in *Hamlet*, 3.1 and 3.4, and for Galatea in Beaumont and Fletcher's *Philaster*, 2.2.[6] They were used for comedy in Jonson's *Volpone*, when Volpone kept peering over or through them while spying on his birds of prey, and in many other plays. Whenever the central opening had to become a town's gates (see below, Chapter 5b), with the defenders on the balcony above, the hangings would have served in place of real doors or gates. If doors had been hung in the central space they would have had to be kept open for most of the time, and would have got in the way of backstage movement.

The central opening or 'discovery space' behind the hangings was often used to display other props, particularly when the opening was meant to show a cell or study. Such uses required a table and chair, and appropriate devices on the table. A stage direction in a Red Bull play, Dekker's *If It Be Not Good, the Devil Is In It*, calls for '*A table ... set out with a candle burning, a deaths head a cloke and a crosse*'. A candle for light (and life), a cloak for the traveller, a skull for human mortality, and the emblem of Christianity, delivered a lot of signals about what was to follow.

Another fixed feature of the early stages that served in some plays was the machinery that backed the use of the traps in the stage floor and the heavens. Smoke and fireworks could be emitted from the trap in the stage platform, for the mists that accompany the masque in Beaumont and Fletcher's *The Maid's Tragedy* and Marlowe's Faustus being dragged down to hell. The risk of fire in wooden playhouses did not stop the players from using the trapdoor as a hell's mouth, with its accompanying shows of brimstone and flame. Henslowe's lists include '1 Hell mought' and '1 dragon in fostes' (Marlowe's *Dr Faustus*), both of which needed an accompaniment with fireworks. Similarly spectacular effects could emerge from the higher trap, too. Shakespeare gave 'Jove's bird, the Roman eagle', who descends from the heavenly trap-door in *Cymbeline*, 5.5, in Posthumus's dream, a firecracker to throw as a thunderbolt. The full stage direction reads '*Jupiter descends in Thunder and Lightning, sitting uppon an Eagle. Hee throws a thunder-bolt.*' What he threw was an explosive firecracker, because when he is drawn back up into the heavens an observer comments 'He came in thunder. His celestial breath | Was sulphurous to smell.' The stench of gunpowder made these devices more congenial in the open-air venues, and despite expressions of disgust by the writers of the indoor play-houses, the bolder playwrights did not hesitate to demand them. Thomas Heywood, writing for the Red Bull in 1610, ordered for the end of one spectacular scene in *The Silver Age*, '*fire-workes all over the house*'.

Both kinds of trapdoor had some kind of machinery backing their use, one for descents and the other for ascents. A stage direction specifies '*suddenly riseth up a great tree*' in the dumbshow of *A Warning for Fair Women*, an anonymous play staged by Shakespeare's company at the end of the 1590s. Whether there was any kind of lift other than stairs to help characters like *Hamlet*'s ghost up onto the stage we cannot be sure, but we do know that there was a windlass in the heavens which allowed the smaller boy players to make descents on a 'creaking throne'. Jupiter in *Cymbeline*, and Juno in *The Tempest*, 4.1, were both lowered slowly down towards the stage, and then drawn up again.

Besides the many smaller and more readily portable properties such as weapons, digging tools, torches, papers as letters or maps, items of clothing like gloves or gauntlets, and special plants like Ophelia's herbs in *Hamlet*, there were a few special cases, notably Fluellen's leek in *Henry V.* The leek is a seasonal vegetable, usually available only from May till October. It is possible that whenever *Henry V* was staged in the winter a leek made of paper for Pistol to chew would have had to replace it.

A 'bank' or flower-covered bench was specified for *A Midsummer Night's Dream*, for instance, and a set of stocks for *King Lear.* Henslowe had similar assets, since he lists two moss banks. Wooden coffins for victims like Ophelia were put to frequent use. Henslowe had two in his list. Other devices provided services which are more conjectural. Henslowe's lists have an item '1 frame for the heading in Black Jone' which might have been the sort of apparatus shown in Reginald Scot's *Discovery of Witchcraft* to produce conjuring tricks in which a decapitated body could be shown with a separate and still-talking head.[7] The listing of such items in the surviving playtexts suggests that the companies acquired such special resources only slowly, but that as time went on their storerooms, especially those of the King's Men at the Globe and the Blackfriars, accumulated a quite substantial variety of devices.

Spectacle and shock effects had their uses throughout the period. Stage blood, usually from a bladder or glass full of pig's blood, was by no means a rare resource. Three such glasses are called for in a scene in a play staged at the Rose, George Peele's *The Battle of Alcazar*, when three characters are disembowelled on stage. According to the bookkeeper's manuscript 'plot', he had to supply '3 violls of blood & a sheeps gather', that is, three pieces of sheep's entrail, the liver, heart and lungs, one for each corpse, along with an appropriate flow of blood from each victim, for display to the excited multitude. Henslowe listed several properties in the form of bodies, including a heifer, 'the limes [limbs] dead', plus 'Faetones [Phaeton's] lymes', and a bear skin and a lion skin. He also noted several heads, including one for the three-headed dog Cerberus, and 'Kentes woden leage'. Faustus needed a separate head, too, for his fake decapitation in the 1616 text, which has a stage direction '*Enter Faustus with the false head*'. Shakespeare's company must have kept Burbage's head in effigy, for the hero's decapitation at the end of *Macbeth*. Cloten's head was presented on stage in *Cymbeline*, 4.2, in this case along with Cloten's headless corpse.

c. Were There Any Special Properties?

The bareness of the Elizabethan stage has been a matter of much debate over the years. Even the colourful painting of the *frons scenae*, which followed the Tudor habit of decorating everything on show, and Hamlet's reference to what was over his head in the stage heavens 'fretted with golden fire', has been doubted. The stage was thickly painted, its scheme of decoration symbolic, reflecting the standard mode of decor applied to every domestic and civic scene in England. But it was bare in that it lacked any scenery or devices to fix a sense of location other than the standard portable props. It was simply a space for walking over, whether it was meant to depict an indoor scene or one out of doors. With very few exceptions its scenes were fixed by word-painting rather than scene-painting.

In general, the conditions of early staging were hostile to special effects and to the use of any special structures. Staging a different play each afternoon meant that there was little time to build a specific set or a special structure for any one play. Anything truly demanding, like the large scaffold that Barabbas uses hammers and ropes to build in the last Act of Marlowe's *The Jew of Malta* to catch the Turkish caliph, was a rare event. The play was performed at the Rose by every company that used it between 1592 and 1595, unlike the other popular Marlowe plays like *Tamburlaine* and *Faustus*, which went with their companies. Conceivably the special demands it laid down for staging made the companies leave it behind in London when they took to the road. Large structures were not readily portable, and took more time to erect and to dismantle than the companies could afford.

Antony and Cleopatra is exceptional amongst the plays that Shakespeare wrote for his company in that it appears to demand a special construction specifically for one scene in the play. The economy with which he ran his own affairs was probably reflected in what he asked for from his fellows. The so-called 'monument' scene, 4.16, the last of the rapid sequence of scenes in Act 4, is unique in the Shakespeare canon in that it seems to have demanded a special structure to stage the first of the play's two tragic deaths.

Shakespeare stuck closely to his main source, Plutarch, for almost all the details in his play. He managed to dodge most of the staging problems such fidelity gave him, with scenes set on ships, a naval battle, and the many exchanges (handled largely by a plethora of messengers) between Egypt and Rome. Plutarch, however, made a great deal of the monument scene, and in this one case Shakespeare chose to follow him closely. It would be nice to know whether the story had such potency for him that for once he chose to present his fellows with the challenge and expense of providing a special structure for it, or whether he saw an easy way to do it merely with what the Globe's *frons scenae* provided.

Plutarch painted the scene in vivid terms. North's translation reads

When he heard that she was alive, he very earnestly prayed his men to carry his body thither; and so he was carried in his men's arms into the entry of the monument. Notwithstanding, Cleopatra would not open the gates, but came to the high windows, and cast out certain chains and ropes, in the which Antonius was trussed; and Cleopatra her owne self, with two women only, which she had suffered to come with her into these monuments, triced Antonius up.

They that were present to behold it said they never saw so pitiful a sight. For they plucked up poor Antonius, all bloody as he was and drawing on with pangs of death, who holding up his hands to Cleopatra raised up himself as well as he could. It was a hard thing for these women to do, to lift him up. But Cleopatra stooping down with her head, putting to all her strength to her uttermost power, did lift him up with much ado and never let go her hold, with the help of the women beneath that bade her be of good courage, and were as sorry to see her labour so, as she herself.[8]

Such a vividly visualized scene may have proved irresistible, whatever the difficulties it created for the carpenters and the musclepower of the boys who were playing the women. Those struggles are nothing compared to the struggles that theatre historians have had in trying to conceive what was originally done to stage them.

The raw evidence in the stage directions is fairly specific. In the Folio text, the only version with any relation to the original playscript, the scene starts with dying Antony being brought onto the main stage to '*Cleopatra and her Maides, aloft*', that is, on the stage balcony. He asks for a last kiss, but she refuses to come down to him, 'Least I be taken'. So he has to go up to her. 'Helpe me my women, we must draw thee up', she says. Then, to 'Heere's sport indeede: | How heavy weighes my Lord?', and 'Oh come, come, come,' they haul on the ropes, and the stage direction says '*They heave Anthony aloft to Cleopatra*'. The dying speeches follow, and the Act ends with '*Exeunt, bearing of Anthonies body*'. Ideas about how this was interpreted on the original Globe stage have ranged from conceiving a special construction, a 'booth', a tent or funeral monument made of wood and cloth, set up just for this scene, to the three boys playing Cleopatra, Charmian, and Iras simply standing on the stage balcony and hauling Antony's body up to it from stage level. A specially-made booth could have been reused for 5.2 when Cleopatra and her maids are using the monument to shelter from Caesar, and Cleopatra is tricked into talk by Proculeius while the soldiers sneak up from behind and capture her. It might even be thought that the top of the monument was the main stage platform, and that Antony was brought in from the yard, where the Roman soldiers later come in to catch Cleopatra. The chief evidence cited in support of this reading is Diomedes saying 'Looke out o'th other side your Monument', which seems to suggest that it had sides, like the main stage, while the linear balcony clearly did not. The trouble with this theory is first, that there is no evidence anywhere in the plays for players ever getting access to the stage from the yard, and secondly that the 'aloft' used in the stage direction about Antony's body was the usual term for the balcony in the tiring-house front. It was not beyond the capacity of Elizabethan imaginations to take Diomedes's reference to the 'other side' as a signal about the fictional four-sided design of the monument.

We have to choose between a maximal, cinematic-minded construction, or a minimal use of the balcony relying on the muscular power of three teenaged boys to draw the body of Antony, bound to a sick-chair or his shield, up to the stage's upper level. Nine feet, plus the height of the balusters, was no small distance to pull a heavy adult torso up vertically, even one that was not strapped to a frame of any kind. And then would Antony have been laid on the balcony's floor for his dying speeches, out of sight behind the balustrade? What could justify the conclusion that this whole scene was staged in the small balcony space, leaving the vast space of the main platform below empty?

Against all these difficulties, we would invoke the minimalist solution to the question, and reject the argument that any special and unique construction was built just for this play. Instead we would invoke the 'sick chair', a stock device for holding sick people, like the one on which John of Gaunt is conveyed in *Richard II*, 2.1. It could hold Antony conveniently seated, both for hauling him up and for setting him down to speak his last speeches with his head still visible over the balcony. The three boys and the seated Antony do not form a larger number than other scenes using the stage balcony, which could hold five or more characters at once. And the main stage was not left empty. Diomedes and the other guards who bring Antony on remain watching the scene above them. They are the '*All*' who aptly exclaim 'A heavy sight' when he reaches the balcony. They are given no exit direction other than the general one at the end of the scene. The boys must have practised hauling Burbage up twelve feet using just ropes and a lot of breath, carefully acknowledged in the dialogue. Dover Wilson, the editor who proposed a timber and canvas 'tent' for the monument, suggested that the heavenly windlass was brought into use to help them. An early direction written for a play staged at the Rose indicates that it could have been used for such a purpose. But Cleopatra's breathless words show that such a wimpish device was no part of Shakespeare's own conception of how the scene was to be staged. He saw Plutarch's description of the scene, and expected his players to live up to it by exploiting the fixed features of the architecture that they were accustomed to using on the Globe's stage.

Henslowe's lists of special properties on the whole endorse this conclusion about minimal staging. His lists do include a few tantalizing references, for instance to 'the sittie of Rome', which may have been a scenic panorama, but is more likely to have been a painted cloth for use as a set of stage hangings, to amplify the scene in which Faustus plays tricks on the Pope, whose 'miter' is also in the Henslowe lists. Every one of the other items in the list of properties which belonged to the Admiral's Men in 1598 was thoroughly portable.

d. Weapons and Fighting

The open-air playhouses were regularly used for noisy combats with swords, the Tudor equivalent of boxing matches. In Jonson's *Epicene, or The Silent Woman*, staged at the Whitefriars in 1609, the chief gull Morose, who hates any kind of noise, speaks gloomily of the dreadful prospect of having to sit through 'a play, that were nothing but fights at sea, drum, trumpet and target'. The firing of chambers from the stage heavens and the noisy accompaniments of military combats by the army's instruments for giving signals on the battlefield, drums and trumpets, conjoined with loud blows of swords on metal shields or targets, was the kind of theatrical uproar he hated. A similar kind of uproar took place on the open stages for more serious purposes than playgoing. Swordfights, whether serious challenges or as 'exhibitions', were almost as popular as animal-baiting, and used similar outdoor venues. The Southwark playhouses in particular were popular for such public shows of prowess. Henslowe records a debt of forty shillings in 1598 for hiring the Rose for a 'challenge', noting that 'James cranwigge the 4 of november 1598 playd his callenge in my howsse & I sholde have had for my parte xxxxs which the company hath rd & oweth yt to me'.[9] John Manningham recorded in his *Diary* for February 1602 that in an exhibition bout at the Swan the professional fencer Dun had been killed by a thrust in the eye.[10] Certainly when the players staged their own bouts on the same stages in play-battles or duels, their games of imitation were judged with a professional eye.

Much has been made of the need for skill at swordplay amongst the early players. The famous clown Richard Tarlton was a Master of Fence, a title for which candidates had to qualify by defeating eleven other Masters in single combat on the same day. How many, even of the leading players, might have had such skills is uncertain. Most of the battle scenes demanded muscle and noise rather than skill. In a post-Restoration play, *Knavery in all Trades*, possibly by John Tatham, a writer for the Red Bull company in 1640, a character tells a nostalgic anecdote about Richard Fowler, the swashbuckling hero of the Fortune playhouse in the 1630s. Still staging old military plays such as *Tamburlaine*, Fowler was famous for the vigour with which his sword clanged on his enemies' shields.

Fowler you know was appointed for the Conquering parts, and it being given out that he was to play the Part of a great Captain and mighty Warriour, drew much Company; the Play began, and ended with his Valour; but at the end of the Fourth Act he laid so heavily about him, that some Mutes who stood for Souldiers, fell down as they were dead e're he had toucht their trembling Targets; so he brandisht his Sword and made his Exit; ne're minding to bring off his dead men; which they perceiving, crauld into the Tyreing house, at which, *Fowler* grew angry and told 'em, Dogs you should have laine there till you had been fetcht off; and so they crauld out again, which gave the People such an occasion of Laughter, they cry'd that again, that again, that again.[11]

None the less, the skills of the leading players should not be under-rated. Duels were entirely affairs of skill, and were played before expert judges. And to accidentally disable any leading player with a clumsy blow could literally damage the company's fortunes. Even the best-armoured shoulder could take hurt from an over-enthusiastic swash.

Broadly speaking, the plays staged two different fighting traditions with two different kinds of weapon. Until the rapier became popular towards the end of the sixteenth century, swords were mainly used for cutting with the blade rather than thrusting with the point. 'Foining', or thrusting with the point, a term that Falstaff and others misused as a sexual joke, was seen by the earlier Tudors as cowardly. They preferred the virtue of a strong right arm which could beat down the opposition with a slashing blow. In Shakespeare's time the military weapons were swords with cutting edges. Coming into favour in the 1580s, the rapier was a weapon for the Englishman Italianate, dangerous because foreign and new-fangled. It was used exclusively for thrusting. Consequently on-stage battle scenes were fought with cutting swords, while for duels in plays like *Hamlet* or *A Fair Quarrel* rapiers became the weapon.

A class and fashion distinction lay behind this division. Generally, on stage the lower-class characters had cutting swords for use in battles, along with metal shields (small hand-held bucklers, the larger targets on the forearm, and occasionally perhaps a full-sized wooden shield protecting the whole arm) and axes, all for swashing blows, plus long pikes or halberds for longer-range thrusting, while the gentry used rapiers in single-combat duello. Metal armour, certainly on the head, neck, arms and chest, was an essential part of this apparatus, to protect the players in such skirmishes. Henslowe records one pair of distinctly odd weapons, '1 wooden hatchet, 1 leather hatchet', which may have had hard leather in place of metal axe-heads as an alternative form of insurance against over-enthusiastic hits.[12] The likelihood that battles were fought with battleaxes as well as with broadswords suggests that serious cuts were a real danger. Combats using rapiers offered quite different kinds of danger. In all exhibition fights and on stage thrusting weapons had 'bated' or blunted points to limit the risk of penetration.

It is not always easy to be sure from the references in the plays which sort of weapon the writers expected the players to use. Shakespeare employed the terms 'sword' and 'rapier' almost interchangeably. In battle scenes especially it is not always clear which sort of weapon the nobility might have used. In general, it can be assumed that battles were fought to show muscle-power and energy, while duels were exhibitions of skill and speed. Hamlet's contest with Laertes was a show of the latest French duelling skills, but Prince Hal most probably fought Douglas and Hotspur in *1 Henry IV* with a broadsword rather than a rapier. In battle the Scottish Douglas at Shrewsbury and Macduff at Dunsinane might have used battleaxes. Such a cutting weapon would certainly have helped Macduff to take off Macbeth's head before he brought it on-stage.

All of the swords, even rapiers, were heavy instruments, taking a lot of strength. Where a modern rapier is no more than half a kilo in total weight, the Elizabethan was more likely to weigh one and a half kilos. Technically the battlefield weapon was usually a 'bastard sword', a thick-bladed, heavy broadsword three feet or more in length, and often with a long hilt for two-handed use. Such a cutting sword, sometimes called a 'fox', was old-fashioned by the turn of the century. In Beaumont and Fletcher's *Philaster*, 4.5, the 'countrey fellow' uses 'my father's old fox' to foil the hero after he has wounded his mistress with his noble rapier. Pistol at Agincourt in *Henry V*, 4.4.9 threatens Monsieur Le Fer with 'point of fox'. His reference to the point of a weapon designed for cutting blows suggests that he was either using it for cowardly 'foining', or simply holding it to the terrified Le Fer's throat to illustrate his threat to 'couple gorge'.

One weapon that may have had value as a symbol of patriotic valour was the staff or stave. Pikes, longstaffs with an iron point, used as a handheld spear, were the most feared and efficient weapon amongst infantry in battle. A fighter with a stave, using its long reach and its weight for giving heavy blows, could defeat a swordsman. It has been suggested that Edgar defeats Oswald in *King Lear* and that Posthumus defeats Iachimo and Belarius and the two boys defeat the Romans in *Cymbeline* by using British staves.[13] In skilful hands, less obviously old-fashioned than the 'fox', a stave or longstaff could show the virtues of country simplicity and of muscle-power.

Henslowe's inventories include quite a variety of weaponry, mostly for battles. Besides the wooden and leather axes, the lists include eight lances, a gilt spear, seventeen foils, one buckler, four wooden targets, nine targets of iron, one of copper, a shield with three lions on it (the insignia for King Richard I), and one helmet 'with a dragon'.[14] In this inventory the term 'foils' appears to signify broadswords and rapiers indifferently. A payment of twenty shillings to 'the armourer' for an unspecified number of new targets was made on 30 September 1602.[15] Armour seems to have counted as apparel rather than as stage properties in these inventories, and is surprisingly absent from the lists. The sole mention of such hardwear is a suit of 'greve armer'.[16] This is a little strange, since the players certainly gave themselves ample upper-body protection with metal and leather. There is no way that they could have enacted their fights, in battle or in single combat, without some fairly substantial protection for their bodies, either of leather or (for preference, given its noise value) of iron. It may be that, as with so many of the ordinary costumes, the players were expected to supply their own items of body armour, so that Henslowe did not need to make much of that sort of provision. The swords were a different matter, because players, not being gentlemen, were not entitled to wear them in the streets. The playhouse had to supply all the items, from clothing to crowns and other signifiers of rank, that belonged to any of the social orders above that of the common player. And that meant pretty well every social rank, from rich citizen to king.

e. Acting

Plays told stories. Each one was the embodiment of a fiction simulated in the appearance of real people. Eloquence of expression, in voice and in body language together, provided colourful words to amplify the narrative which was the essential heart of the play. It was the story, though, that gave the play its shape, its justification, and its 'truth'. While an eloquent speech, Hieronymo's ravings in *The Spanish Tragedy*, the tragic hero's desperate pleading before his death in *Dr Faustus*, or one of Hamlet's soliloquies, were celebrated enough to be noted down in a gallant's notebook of quotable commonplaces, most of the playgoers came to see the enactment of a lurid story. In a high-speed repertory, through a stage traffic of little more than two hours, you did not expect to dwell for long on Hamlet's agonizings about whether anything was to be or not to be, or King Richard's grief over becoming nothing at Pomfret. The players lacked time or reason to indulge themselves in slow and lengthy meditations. Even if their fellows had the patience to wait through such *longueurs*, the ground-lings would not.

There is not very much direct evidence about the style of acting that developed in London from the 1590s onwards. In the early 1600s writers for the boy companies mocked the gestural and vocal excesses of the adults in comparison with the boys, and in the last years the adults at the indoor playhouses mocked the excesses of performers like Richard Fowler at the 'citizen' playhouses, the Fortune and Red Bull. But their attacks were aimed at excessive noise and gesture, not any feature of acting style. Over-acting was a target at different times in every playhouse. Even Burbage in the person of Hamlet in 1600 could condemn the unnatural or 'ab-hominable' excesses of an over-doing adult player. It says little about how naturalistic or stylized the body language of a good player might have been.

The language of gesture has not changed very greatly in the last four hundred years. John Bulwer's *Chirologia* and *Chironomia*, books of hand language written in the early 1640s as a help to the deaf, supply drawings of gestural signs most of which would be recognizable today. An angry man slams his hand down on the table, a beggar holds out his open palm in supplication, a threat is accompanied by the waving of a clenched first, a thinking man scratches his head, and a man ashamed covers his face. A superior offers his or her hand to be kissed, while a man wishing to honour another kisses the extended hand. Enemies when reconciled shake hands. Penitence is expressed by wringing the hands. A blessing is made with upraised hand, showing the palm. The standard gestures that went with fighting, with broadswords, rapiers, staves, cudgels, or axes, were probably not very much less recognizable than these.

Rather less clear is the decorum that went with dress, and especially the language of hats. Its formalities are preserved now chiefly in the armed forces, where salutes are a survival of the stock gesture of respect to a superior, touching the hat as a shrunken relic of the full doffing gesture made to royalty. The rigid social distinctions of Tudor society made doffing to one's superior an absolute necessity. A man speaking to his master kept his hat in his hand throughout the conversation. Replacing the hat immediately after doffing was an assertion of equal status. These distinctions in behaviour reflected the distinctions in dress itself, as attested by the choice of fabric and ornament.

f. Movement on the Early Stages

Most modern thinking about stage movement is still dominated by the two dimensions of proscenium-arch staging. Cinema encourages this, since whatever the depth of focus the camera eye always has a single perspective, and always shows a two-dimensional image. The square stages of the Swan, the Globe, and the Fortune, and most of all the surround of audience, with the gentry positioned at what we think of as the back of the stage platform, demanded a three-dimensional style of acting that modern approaches have largely forgotten.

The essential features of the patterns by which the players walked across the early stages are most clearly demonstrated by what might fairly if ambiguously be called the 'ins and outs' of stage movement. The following chapters (4–6) examine a body of evidence about early staging that is not taken from spectacular events like Hamlet's duel or Cleopatra's struggle to haul Antony's body up onto her monument. Instead they look into a more routine and far more pervasive form of stage movement: the constant business of making entrances and exits. It is possible to find the characteristic practices of the players far more distinctly through their routine activities than through any stage feat specially designed and enacted for a single occasion.

In the process, these chapters will try to show how suspect a seemingly simple stage direction such as '*Exit*' can be. When a curt directive on the page had to be transacted through the course of as many as four lines of speech before the movement was completed, there was ample time for an experienced player to generate some complex but silent stage business as he moved. The study of the business of making entrances and exits in the plays is a feature of the early staging that we ignore at our peril.

The Ins and Outs of Stage Movement

a. What Entry and Exit Stage Directions Indicate

One of the features of early staging only recently recognized is the spread of movement over the large platform stages, and the inadequacy of the simple directions '*Enter*' and '*Exit/Exeunt*' to mark either the space to be covered or the time such moves took. A careful analysis of the entry and exit stage directions in the plays tells us a lot about movement on stage and the positioning of the characters with speaking parts. This chapter looks into what the ins and outs in Shakespeare's plays have to say about stage movement.

In *Hamlet*, 2.2, Hamlet, after hearing the First Player's speech about Pyrrhus killing Priam, instructs Polonius to see the players well treated, and tells him to lead them away. The Q2 text at this point reads as follows:

> *Pol.* My Lord, I will use them according to their desert.
> *Ham.* Gods bodkin man, much better, use every man
> after his desert, & who shall scape whipping, use
> them after your owne honor and dignity, the lesse
> they deserve the more merrit is in your bounty. Take
> them in.
> *Pol.* Come sirs.
> *Ham.* Follow him friends, weele heare a play to morrowe;
> dost thou heare me old friend, can you play the murther
> of *Gonzago?*
> *Play.* I my Lord.

Ham. Weele hate to morrowe night, you could for neede
study a speech of some dosen lines, or sixteene lines,
which I would set downe and insert in't, could you not?
Play. I my Lord.
Ham. Very well, followe that Lord, & looke you mock
him not. My good friends, Ile leave you tell night, you
are welcome to *Elsonoure.* *Exeunt Pol. and Players.*
Ros. Good my Lord. *Exeunt.*
Ham. I so God buy to you, now I am alone,

. . . .

(2.2.529–50)

Q2 makes Polonius and the players depart together after Hamlet's
speech beginning with 'Very well, followe that Lord'. In this passage,
the F1 dialogue is almost the same as Q2, but F1's stage directions give
Polonius a solo exit immediately after his 'Come sirs,' and provide no
exit for the players. Q1 also marks Corambis's [i.e. Polonius's] exit
immediately after the last line he speaks ('Welcome my good fel-
lowes'), and provides no exit for the players.

It is generally agreed that Q2 and F1 were printed from, respectively,
Shakespeare's foul papers and a transcript of the playbook reflecting
Shakespeare's revised version, and that Q1 is a reported text which
reflects performances based on the playbook from which F1 descends.
The *New Cambridge Shakespeare* and the Oxford *Complete Works* adopt
Polonius's early solo exit and add an exit for the players after 'Very well,
followe that Lord, & looke you mock him not.' The Cambridge editor
thinks of the F1 stage direction for Polonius's exit as 'a clear case of the
book-keeper beginning to visualize the staging as he transcribed
Shakespeare's MS'.[1] The Oxford editors insist on the importance of
the independent agreement of Q1 and F1 as a reflection of theatrical
practice.[2] This may be so. But do the Q2 and F1 texts prescribe
different actions in this passage? Did the movements that Polonius
and the players actually made on the Globe stage differ from what
Shakespeare had originally intended in the manuscript Q2 was printed
from?

The dialogue includes speeches which serve as cues for the actors'
movements. These are verbal directions built into the dialogue by
the author, a standard practice which reduced the need for explicit
stage directions. Whether we use Q2 or F1, the dialogue indicates

these movements: Polonius would begin to leave the stage immediately after or while saying 'Come sirs'; the players would turn their backs and begin to walk towards the *frons scenae* in response to Hamlet's 'Follow him friends'; Hamlet then interrupts the First Player's move by saying 'dost thou heare me old friend'; the other players would stop to wait for him, and Polonius in turn would stop to wait for them, although out of earshot. When Hamlet tells the players to follow Polonius for the second time, Hamlet refers to him as 'that Lord', which suggests that Polonius is still visible at that moment, but at a distance. Seeing the players now start to follow him, Polonius would resume his exit, and they would shortly disappear from the stage. Hamlet dismisses Rosencrantz and Guildenstern by saying, 'My good friends, Ile leave you tell night, you are welcome to *Elsonoure*.' They would probably start to go immediately after Rosencrantz says 'Good my Lord' as his farewell, following in the wake of Polonius and the players.

It is not certain whether in his manuscript Shakespeare set the exit stage direction for Polonius and the players just after 'you are welcome to *Elsonoure*' as it is printed in Q2. It seems at least possible that he wrote it to the right of the three-line speech beginning with 'Very well, followe that Lord,' using two or three lines of the margin. In any event, since the Q2 dialogue and the F1 dialogue require the movements suggested above, the Q2 exit stage direction for Polonius and the players, originally written by Shakespeare, is printed in the vicinity of the point where they should finally go out of a stage door, whereas the F1 and Q1 exit stage directions for Polonius, which might be attributed respectively to the book-keeper and the actor-reporter, are placed at or around the point where Polonius should begin to lead the players away. Both Q2 and F1 seem to place the exit of Rosencrantz and Guildenstern at the point where they begin to leave. So far as the exit of Polonius and the players is concerned, despite the disagreement about the placement of the stage directions, the three primary texts provide almost the same action.

This example has important implications. First, in Shakespeare's plays, exits might be interrupted. Secondly, it seems that Shakespeare, the book-keeper, and their fellow actors treated exits as moves which had a certain duration—i.e. moves to be begun, continued, and completed. This implies that some exit stage directions may indicate the beginning of such a process while others may indicate the completion of it.

Other examples give support to this indication that Shakespeare took account of the time needed for exits on the Globe's and similar stages. Towards the end of *King Lear*, 3.7, the blinded Gloucester exits, led by a servant. As the F1 stage direction for their exit indicates, the servant unbinds Gloucester and begins to lead him away immediately after Regan's command: 'Go thrust him out at gates, and let him smell | His way to Dover' (3.7.91–2).[3] Clearly Gloucester is still making his stumbling exit when Cornwall repeats his wife's order two lines later: 'Turne out that eyelesse Villaine' (3.7.94). These harsh words would not only reinforce our sense of Cornwall's cruelty but intensify the painfulness of Gloucester's departure. In *The Two Gentlemen of Verona*, 4.4, the slow-moving Lance would begin to depart just after Proteus's 'Away, I say: stayest thou to vexe me here' (4.4.59), but he is still on stage to be referred to as 'yond foolish Lowt' (4.4.64) about four lines later.

Admittedly, Gloucester's blind exit and Lance's departure with his dog may be exceptionally slow. *The Merchant of Venice* Q1 provides another example, where the exit stage direction clearly indicates the beginning of the departure, but not the actual exit.

> *Bass.* I pray thee good *Leonardo* thinke on this,
> These things being bought and orderly bestowed
> Returne in hast, for I doe feast to night
> My best esteemd acquaintance, hie thee goe.
> *Leon.* My best endevours shall be done heerein.
> *Exit Leonardo.*
> *Enter Gratiano.*
> *Grati.* Where's your Maister.
> *Leonar.* Yonder sir he walkes.
> *Grati.* Signior *Bassanio.*

(2.2.163–9)

As the dialogue requires, Leonardo must move quickly. While walking off but still on stage, he exchanges speeches with the entering character, Gratiano. In reply to Gratiano's question where Bassanio is, Leonardo says, 'Yonder sir he walkes.' The inclusion of 'yonder' or 'yond' in this example and in the passage from *The Two Gentlemen* suggests the distance between the exiting characters and the on-stage characters who have just sent them on their way. The depth of the stage, and the space between the characters at front-stage and the doors in the *frons*, is a measure of the distance that characters entering or exiting had to cover on the early stages.

Although *The Merchant* Q1 is thought to have been printed from Shakespeare's fair copy or a scribal transcript of it, it is certain that the printer's copy had not been polished in all details. It is unlikely that the placing of this exit stage direction is an error or an abandoned but uncorrected first thought by Shakespeare.[4] For one thing, in the early texts of Shakespeare's plays there is a significant number of exit stage directions followed by speeches spoken to the exiting characters. For another, in Shakespeare's plays the situation in which a character leaving exchanges speeches with a newly-arrived character is by no means infrequent. There are relatively few exit stage directions which obviously mark the whole process of beginning and completing an exit. Most commonly it seems that the stage direction '*Exit/Exeunt*' indicates the beginning of a process rather than a single action which is completed immediately.

As with the stage direction '*Exit/Exeunt*', the stage direction '*Enter*' does not always indicate the moment when the actor appears from a stage door or another entry point. In *Much Ado about Nothing* Q1, Borachio's entrance is marked between Don John's 'Who comes here? what newes Borachio?' (1.3.36–8) and Borachio's first speech. In our modern usage of '*Enter*', this placing is completely unacceptable. *Much Ado* Q1 is thought to be a foul-paper text which contains many uncorrected first thoughts by Shakespeare,[5] but the placing of this entrance is neither an abandoned first thought nor an error. In such early texts of Shakespeare's plays, whether printed from foul papers or from playbooks or transcripts, some entry stage directions are placed immediately before the first speeches spoken by the entering characters and some are placed immediately after the speeches spoken to them. Others are placed a few lines before the entering characters either speak or are spoken to. This apparent inconsistency suggests that Shakespeare and his colleagues were used to dealing with entrances as moves which took a length of time.

Hamlet, 5.1 provides an example which might be called a broken entrance. In the Q2 text, the entry stage direction for Hamlet and

Horatio, '*Enter Hamlet and Horatio*', is marked immediately before Hamlet's first speech, 'Has this fellowe no feeling of his busines? a sings in grave-making' (5.1.65–6). In the F1 text, however, the stage direction reading '*Enter Hamlet and Horatio a farre off*' is marked nine lines earlier, i.e. five lines before the First Clown begins to sing. Since Hamlet's first remark implies that he and Horatio have been watching and listening to the First Gravedigger, the Q2 entry stage direction, derived from Shakespeare's foul papers, may have been intended to indicate the point not where Hamlet and Horatio enter but when they should reach the trap which serves as the grave. On the other hand, the F1 entry stage direction, whether Shakespeare or the book-keeper decided its placing, and the added description, '*a farre off*', clearly indicate the moment when they should appear from a stage door. This adverbial phrase seems to suggest that Hamlet and Horatio do not walk directly towards the trap after their arrival.

Most Elizabethan stage directions that include '*afar off*' are for off-stage sound effects. There are relatively few examples where an adverbial phrase such as this is used to describe an on-stage action. These few cases are more or less comparable to the entry stage directions that include '*aloof*', '*aloof off*', '*apart*', '*at a distance*', and the like. In *3 Henry VI* F1, when Margaret, Edward, and Oxford are requested to 'stand aside' (3.3.110), the stage direction for them reads '*They stand aloofe.*' It seems likely that the distance indicated by '*afar off*', '*aloof*', and the like is from centre-stage to the side, rather than from front-stage to back. Since entering characters very often keep their distance in order to observe or overhear on-stage characters, they might have hidden behind stage posts, in the playhouses where posts were available.[6] '*Enter listening/ privately/ unseen/...*' might be treated as variants of '*Enter aloof*'. In *1 Sir John Oldcastle*, a 1599 Rose play, King Harry enters following the traitors and stands by the door he enters by to overhear them: '*Enter Cambridge, Scroope, and Gray, as in a chamber, and set downe at a table, consulting about their treason: King Harry and Suffolke listning at the doore*' (lines 2086–8).[7] Although when this play was performed, the Rose's stage had a covering roof and posts supporting it,[8] Harry was not expected to conceal himself behind one of the stage posts, which at the second Rose appear to have been positioned at the front edge of the stage. Staying by the entrance door and peeping round it would make his overhearing more respectable than hiding behind a post. Entering characters could always keep their 'aloof' distance from on-stage characters by pausing at their entrance and remaining near the entry door. In the case of *Hamlet*, on the Globe stage, Hamlet and Horatio could either have remained near the *frons*, or moved to a side position, or hidden themselves behind a stage post. Since the situation is not tense at all, they probably did not need to use a stage post.

b. How Much Time is Allowed for Exits

It seems most likely that in Elizabethan public playhouses the action usually took place at front-stage to allow the audience positioned on four sides of the stage to see and hear better.[9] Whether the stage was very deep, as at the Globe, or comparatively shallow, as at the Rose, actors clearly needed some length of time to return to the tiring house. Shakespeare, an actor as well as a playwright, a man of the theatre in all senses, was fully aware of this fact.

As You Like It, 1.2 has an especially revealing case. After encouraging Orlando, Rosalind and Celia begin to leave. Three lines later, however, Rosalind stops and restrains Celia from going, saying 'He cals us back' (1.2.241), and approaches Orlando again, probably leaving Celia alone near their exit door. Since Shakespeare wrote *As You Like It* to be performed at the Globe, and he was thoroughly familiar with its stage, the number of lines Orlando is given to deliver between the beginning of Rosalind and Celia's exit and its interruption is significant. Shakespeare might have been aware that if he had given Orlando more than three lines, Rosalind and Celia would have completed their exit. In most modern productions, the actress performing Rosalind dawdles almost into the wings before stopping suddenly and hurrying back to Orlando.[10] This practice is determined by the size and design of modern stages. Other evidence for timing exits shows that the original players of Rosalind and Celia would not necessarily have been required to dawdle. This suggests that even in those instances where the moves of exiting characters are not clearly built into the accompanying dialogue, Shakespeare would have allowed a certain amount of time for the actors to complete their exits. We can estimate the supposed length of time allowed for exits in his plays through the number of lines delivered by other characters while the exiters are walking to one of the two (or three) doors in the *frons*.[11]

A number of mid-scene exits and mid-scene entrances are correlated in the sense that the completion of the former is required for the latter to be made. Therefore the number of lines delivered between beginning an exit and an entrance relating to that exit includes at the least all the lines delivered between the beginning and completion of the exit. Examining the instances with the fewest lines tells us how much time was usually allowed for exits. They can be divided into the following patterns:

A   A character exits and re-enters.

A^+ A character exits to fetch something and re-enters with it.[12]

B   A character exits to summon another character, and the summoned character enters either alone or with the summoner.

These patterns include only instances where the exit and its related entrance are both made on the main stage, leaving aside those in which an ascent to the upper playing level by the exiter himself is involved, or those in which the exit is made from the upper playing level. Although pattern A^+ is a variant of pattern A, it could be combined with pattern B, for these patterns share a potent feature: the exit itself presages its related entrance.

We have searched the early printed texts of Shakespeare's plays for instances of each pattern. It would be unreasonable to rely very much upon stage directions to determine when characters begin to exit or when they enter through one of the stage doors. Instead, we have to look for the primary basis for deciding on the moments when the exits and entrances begin. These have to be found in the speeches themselves.

Usually in Shakespeare's plays an exit is denoted in the dialogue—through an intention to depart spoken by the exiter himself, an instruction or request from another character telling or asking the exiter to depart, or something similar. Such lines serve primarily as cues for the actor to begin to exit. As a rule, therefore, we have identified the beginnings of exits just after these 'exit cues'. Where there is a stage direction indicating a different point of exit we have accepted that point as an alternative possibility, unless it is unreasonable to assume that the exiter begins to leave at the point. In some cases a character's exit is not indicated either by an 'exit cue' or by an exit stage direction, but is implied only by the fact that the character re-enters later. In such cases we have looked for something that can serve as a cue for his exit, no matter how vague a cue it may be, such as a noise made within or a speech delivered by, or spoken to, the character. In accordance with this, we would for instance place the beginning of Bardolph's exit and that of Seyton's at *2 Henry IV*, 2.4.371 and at *Macbeth*, 5.5.8 respectively.[13]

In Shakespeare's plays, an entrance is usually announced through a speech spoken by, or to, the enterer, or by a short speech referring to his approach. We may reasonably believe that entrances came before such 'entry announcements'. In the majority of cases entry stage directions are placed just before such speeches, not only in texts based upon Shakespeare's copies or scribal transcripts of them but also in texts based upon playbooks or scribal transcripts of them. For example, in *Macbeth* F1, which is based upon a playhouse manuscript, there are forty-four mid-scene entry stage directions, thirty-seven of which are placed just before 'entry announcements'. Some extant non-Shakespearian playhouse manuscripts do show that book-keepers occasionally marked entry stage directions some lines before such points. Here it is assumed that their intention was to allow enterers time to join on-stage characters just before they first speak or are addressed.[14] In Fredson Bowers's view, in any printed (or manuscript) text, it is a convention that a character's entrance is marked just before he speaks, whereas in performance his entrance must have been made slightly earlier.[15] If so, there must be a considerable number of instances in which we should locate the entrance in the text some lines before the enterer first speaks or is addressed, in spite of the position of the entry stage direction. In practice it is impossible to judge how many lines earlier the entrance should be placed in each particular case. Accordingly, we generally locate entrances just before 'entry announcements', and where there is an entry stage direction indicating an earlier point, we accept that point as an alternative possibility, unless it is clear that the stage direction is absolutely misplaced.

One clear-cut instance is in *The Taming of the Shrew*:

> *Hor.* Sirra *Biondello*, goe and intreate my wife to come to
> me forthwith.   *Exit. Bion.*

Pet. Oh ho, intreate her, nay then shee must needes come.
Hor. I am affraid sir, doe what you can
              Enter Biondello.
Yours will not be entreated: Now, where's my wife?
Bion. Shee saies you have some goodly Jest in hand,
She will not come: she bids you come to her.
                      (*The Taming of the Shrew,* 5.2.91–7)

The F1 text of *The Taming of the Shrew* was printed either from
Shakespeare's foul papers or from a transcript of them which had
undergone some minor theatrical adaptation. It is certain that Biondello begins to exit in response to Hortensio's instruction at the end
of 5.2.92, where the stage direction for his exit is placed. On the
other hand, although he is first addressed in the middle of 5.2.95
('Now, where's my wife?'), the stage direction for his entrance is
placed at 5.2.94 (in the middle of Hortensio's sentence, 'I am affraid
sir, doe what you can…'). The entry stage direction seems to be
marked half a line too early. Does that half line allow Biondello to
approach Hortensio? If the entry stage direction was originally Shakespeare's, it was probably placed in his foul papers at the end of line 94.
Either just after he wrote the sentence comprising line 94 and the
first half of line 95, or more probably just after he wrote lines 94–5,
which are prefixed by a single speaker's name, Shakespeare marked the
entry stage direction to the right of line 94 at least partly because
sufficient space was left there for it. However, if the entry stage
direction was originally the book-keeper's, rather than Shakespeare's,
the F1 placement of it may have resulted from the book-keeper's usual
practice of marking his annotations beside speeches in the left or
right margin of the copy received from the author. In this case he
would have had no choice but to place the entry stage direction either
to the left of line 95 or to the right of line 94, even if he thought that the
middle of line 95 was the proper moment for Biondello's entrance. The
positioning of the entry stage direction therefore does not necessarily
mark the exact point at which Biondello was supposed to enter. We
have therefore tentatively concluded that Biondello re-enters with his
message from the Widow in the middle of 5.2.95, while conceding the
possibility that he re-enters at 5.2.94. This instance (*The Taming of the
Shrew,* 5.2.92–5m[94]) we count as an instance of pattern A$^+$ in which

the number of lines for the exit and re-entry is two and a half or just two.

The early texts of Shakespeare's plays depend on manuscript copy of various kinds. The examples mentioned above of the three patterns may in part reflect the nature of the particular text which provides them. For our examples of the three patterns, when the plays exist in two or three kinds of text, we have used whichever texts seem closest to the playbook of Shakespeare's company. Judging from a comparison of the substantive texts of each play, the influence of the text on the data concerning the play is not crucial, whether it is based on Shakespeare's copy or a scribal transcript of it or based on the playbook or a scribal transcript of it, and whether the text contains evidence of Shakespeare's revisions or not. Comparing the Q1, Q2, and F1 texts of *Hamlet*, for instance, shows that reported texts are not helpful in identifying the length of exit times. With the exception of *Pericles*, therefore, there is no need to use such a text when assembling examples.

Our sample (see Table 1) comprises all the examples found in Shakespeare's plays, including *Pericles*. We have only excluded those instances in which a sound or an action fills the gap between the beginning of the exit and the entrance. Therefore such examples as *King Lear*, 5.2.4–4 (Edgar's exit and re-entrance) and *Hamlet*, 3.2.129–129 (the Player Queen's and Player Lucianus's exits and re-entrances) are not counted as instances of no lines. Where two or more examples share the same exit or entrance, we have counted the one where the number of lines is smallest. For example, Charmian's exit when she brings in a messenger (*Antony and Cleopatra*, 2.5.81–4m) has been

Table 1. Number of instances of each pattern

Pattern	Number of lines										
	0	1	2	3	4	5	6	7	8	9	10
A	0	0	0	4	8	2	7	5	8	3	4
A+	2	3	2	4	3	4	5	3	3	2	1
B	9	5	13	11	12	10	4	4	7	8	1
Total	11	8	15	19	23	16	16	12	18	13	6

Note: In this table, extra part-lines are counted as full lines.

included, but not the instance where the messenger exits and re-enters with her (*Antony and Cleopatra*, 2.5.74–84m).[16] Lastly, we have included a few doubtful examples where it is not certain whether the exit and entrance are really correlated, or whether the exit and entrance both actually occur.

The examples where the number of lines is small are important for this purpose, so in Table 1 we show the number of instances of each pattern in which the number of lines is between nought and ten. Eleven instances have no lines, but the majority of these are doubtful or controversial examples. There are only a few real instances in which the number of lines is none or one, but in the great majority of cases the number of lines is two or more. It can safely be concluded that in Shakespeare's plays characters are generally allowed at least two lines to complete their exits.

In the case of pattern A, although there are no instances where the number is less than two, in a few cases there are three, and there are several where the number is four.[17] All the exiters who require three lines, namely, Whitmore in *2 Henry VI*, the First Murderer in *Richard III*, Catesby in *Richard III*, and Bardolph in *2 Henry IV*, are subordinate or minor characters, while some exiters in the instances where the number of lines is four (Titus, Mistress Ford, Othello, and Lear) are major characters. In these cases it is worth noting that Whitmore and the First Murderer do not exit alone but with major characters, Suffolk and Clarence. In neither case does the text provide anything to suggest from what part of the stage the exiter begins to leave, but since they accompany major characters, it is unlikely that they have been standing apart by the *frons scenae*. These figures indicate that characters with speaking parts were usually allowed about four lines, and occasionally about three, to walk from the main acting area, i.e. front-stage, to one of the two (or three) stage doors.

There is no important difference between the distribution of instances of pattern A^+ and pattern B. In pattern A^+, while there are no reliable zeros, and only one one-line case, there are a few in which the number of lines is two; in pattern B, there are several reliable instances where there are none or one, and many in which the number of lines is two. Where both patterns have between none and two, almost all the exiters are minor characters, such as servants and attendants. The reason why such minor characters are usually allowed two lines or less to complete their exits is that their acting area is ordinarily the rear of the stage, nearest the doors, and they are expected to move off very quickly.

Exiters who were allowed only one line or less were all expected to begin their exits from positions by the *frons scenae* and near the doors. Characters who neither speak nor are addressed until they are told to pursue off-stage business, such as the knight (*King Lear*, 1.4.46–7 (A^+ = 1)) and the attendant (*2 Henry VI*, 5.1.145–145 (B = 0)), were possibly meant to stand near the stage doors while on stage. Those who enter only to announce that other characters are waiting off-stage to make their entrances and who exit to summon them immediately, such as the Hostess (*1 Henry IV*, 2.5.511–511 (B = 0)) and Dennis (*As You Like It*, 1.1.89–90 (B = 1)), quite naturally would stand by the doors through which they have entered during their very short presence on the stage. Each of the doubtful instances gives support to this conclusion. In the case of *All's Well That Ends Well*, 2.1.90–1 (B = 1), in particular, it is unlikely that Lafew would begin his exit from an extreme rear position, for he exchanges speeches for some thirty lines with the King of France, the central character in *All's Well*, 2.1, before he begins to move.[18] It seems reasonable to conclude that he does not really leave the stage, but only walks a few paces towards a stage door, and beckons the newcomer Helen to enter once he can see through it.

This evidence shows that major characters are usually allowed about four lines to complete their exits, while minor characters are ordinarily allowed no more than two. The major characters must normally occupy a front-stage position, and so have further to walk to their exit doors. This deduction provides a framework allowing us to assess the form of each kind of exit individually.

c. What Happens While Entrances and Exits are being made

If in Shakespeare's plays characters are usually allowed about four lines to return to the tiring house from the front of the stage, it makes sense to conclude that the same number of lines must have been allowed for entering characters to reach front-stage. Making a four-line entrance or exit allows a considerable opportunity for special effects.

Antony and Cleopatra, 1.1 is a visibly artificial scene. It begins and ends with two Roman soldiers, Philo and Demetrius. Their task is to provide the framework within which Antony and Cleopatra make their first appearance and speak of their love. Philo and Demetrius are presenters or commentators, standing on one side of the stage. While Philo is speaking of Antony's 'dotage', he and Cleopatra enter with their trains. After perceiving their arrival, Philo speaks three and a half lines:

> Looke where they come:
> Take but good note, and you shall see in him
> (The triple Pillar of the world) transform'd
> Into a Strumpets Foole. Behold and see.

> (1.1.10–13)

These lines fill the time it takes for the hero and heroine to walk forward from the entrance door so that they can deliver their important speeches at the front of the stage. Philo also draws the audience's attention to their entrance and invites the audience to view Antony's state from his Roman point of view, although Antony and Cleopatra themselves, through their words and their behaviour to each other, show that there is another point of view about their love.

The moment Antony and Cleopatra begin to leave the stage, Demetrius and Philo resume their conversation.

> *Dem.* Is *Caesar* with *Anthonius* priz'd so slight?
> *Philo.* Sir sometimes when he is not *Anthony*,
> He comes too short of that great Property
> Which still should go with *Anthony*.

> (1.1.58–61)

If these four lines are spoken while the lovers are still on stage, walking towards the tiring house, they would effectively serve as a critical comment on Antony's action of leaving with Cleopatra, ignoring the messenger from Caesar. Antony and Cleopatra are utterly indifferent to the dialogue between Philo and Demetrius. The speakers, for their part, seem equally unconcerned whether Antony and Cleopatra hear them or not, despite the fact that in both examples severe criticism is made of the two protagonists while they are on stage and, at least notionally, in earshot. In neither case do the lines in question cause the audience to wonder if Antony and Cleopatra hear them.

These are examples of speeches whose meanings and effects cannot be fully appreciated unless the audience hear them as they register the entrances and exits which are made while they are being spoken. The text always needs to be read as a component of the staging, most particularly when it concerns speeches around entrances and exits.

Romeo and Juliet, 2.2 provides a well-known example of an early entrance. Q2 marks Romeo's entrance eight lines before he speaks. The intervening eight lines were presumably intended to be delivered while Romeo is walking towards the Friar and the attention of the audience is partly on Romeo's presence and approach. Since eight lines is a considerable length of time, it may be that he walks very slowly, or else he stops a few lines after his arrival and resumes his move later. The previous scene, 2.1, concludes with Romeo's exit, which is accompanied by his speech indicating his intention to visit the Friar: 'Hence will I to my ghostly Friers close cell, | His helpe to crave, and my deare hap to tell' (2.1.233–4). These lines would prepare the audience to identify the Friar as the character whom Romeo is shortly to visit. The Friar on his entrance has to establish the atmosphere or mood in which Romeo is received. The Friar speaks of the ambivalence of things such as plants, herbs, and stones, and refers to the parallelism between herbs and man, that is to say, the ambivalence of the nature of man, while Romeo is walking towards him. Thus the eight lines in question can serve as a comment on the situation in which Romeo now finds himself, implying that Romeo's 'dear hap' may possibly turn out to be his mishap.[19] It is the Friar's task to introduce a tragic viewpoint into the play, since up to this point the comic mood has been predominant, and to suggest that the hero has actually begun to follow the tragic course of which the Chorus spoke in the Prologue. In a sense the Friar has taken over the Chorus's function.[20] The effect of his speech is more like direct comment than ironic circumlocution. Alan C. Dessen suggests that 'a Romeo who hears the friar talking about the presence of both poison and medicine within the same flower may be more likely to think of such poison (and the apothecary) in 5.1'.[21] We think it at least questionable whether the fact that Romeo arrives in the middle of the Friar's speech means that he overhears him, although the audience was certainly expected to see the connections.

When a character exits to summon another character, the summoner's exit itself presages the entrance of the summoned character, so the lines between the beginning of the summoner's exit and the entrance of the summoned character are delivered while the audience anticipates the entrance of the summoned character. In *Hamlet*, 4.5, for example, Gertrude speaks the following four lines after having told Horatio to let Ophelia come in.

> To my sicke soule (as sinnes true Nature is)
> Each toy seemes Prologue, to some great amisse,
> So full of Artlesse jealousie is guilt,
> It spill's it selfe, in fearing to be spilt.

> (4.5.17-20)

Most modern editions indicate that these lines are an aside. It is possible that Horatio does not really exit but just opens a stage door to admit Ophelia. In any event, whether he really exits or not, if he needs about four lines to reach the door, he is on stage while Gertrude is speaking her four. We may doubt, however, whether Gertrude cares if Horatio hears her or not. She strongly feels a premonition of a grievous occurrence—her heart filled with grief and guilt—so that she is completely unaware of Horatio's presence. Furthermore, it seems that what the audience is expected to do while hearing the four lines is to prepare themselves, as Gertrude is doing, to receive the entrance of Ophelia, rather than to enter into Gertrude's feelings, or to wonder if Horatio hears her. It is certain that the lines can serve as the 'prologue' to the episode in which the distracted Ophelia performs.

In *King Lear*, 4.5, Lear has scarcely begun to exit when an anonymous gentleman speaks a four-line speech.

> A sight most pittifull in the meanest wretch,
> Past speaking of in a King. Thou hast a Daughter
> Who redeemes Nature from the generall curse
> Which twaine have brought her to.

> (4.5.200-3)

Lear probably completes his exit before the gentleman finishes delivering these four lines, since he exits running. However, it is obvious that they serve as a comment on Lear's exit, telling the audience that however pitiful the appearance of his exit may be, it will lead to the reunion scene in which Lear's broken heart will be healed by his loving daughter, Cordelia.

Alan C. Dessen has suggested that, in certain instances, despite the stage direction '*Exeunt (omnes)*', the exiters may leave separately and a few lines apart.[22] The closing *Exeunt* of *Julius Caesar*, 2.2 is a likely example.

> *Caes.* Bid them prepare within:
>   I am too blame to be thus waited for.
>   Now *Cynna*, now *Metellus:* what *Trebonius*,
>   I have an houres talke in store for you:
>   Remember that you call on me to day:
>   Be neere me, that I may remember you.
> *Treb.* *Caesar* I will: and so neere will I be,
>   That your best Friends shall wish I had beene further.
> *Caes.* Good Friends go in, and taste some wine with me
>   And we (like Friends) will straight way go together.
> *Bru.* That every like is not the same, O *Caesar*,
>   The heart of *Brutus* earnes to thinke upon.   *Exeunt*
>
> (2.2.118–29)

The dialogue seems to suggest that Caesar begins to exit with others just before Brutus's speech. It is likely that the concluding two lines of 2.2 are intended to be spoken while Caesar is exiting with his 'friends'. These lines not only indicate that, unlike the other conspirators, Brutus is in deep grief over Caesar's tragic fortune but also serve as a comment on Caesar's exit, telling the audience that Caesar is moving towards his death because of the confidence he magnanimously has in his 'friends'. It may be a matter of indifference to Brutus whether or not Caesar hears him. It seems that unlike Trebonius's words ('and so neere will I be, . . .') Brutus's speech is more a soliloquy than an aside.

We do not, of course, wish to suggest that every speech delivered around an entrance or exit serves as a comment upon that entrance or exit. What we should like to emphasize is that speeches around entrances and exits are more often than not highly theatrical, and that they therefore rarely lend themselves to a literal-minded or 'realistic' interpretation. Presumably some convention operated on the Shakespearian stage concerning the relationship between on-stage characters and entering or exiting characters. Shakespearian actors and audiences knew that when a character turns his back and begins to move towards the tiring house, the character is assumed to move out of earshot. Their understanding was that the character would have already stopped playing a part in the dialogue. On the other hand, since an entering character normally faces front-stage, the convention here may not always be open to a simple explanation. Even so, an entering character can easily give the impression of not being ready to become involved in the dialogue. In our view, unless the entering character makes any direct response to the on-stage character's speech, the Elizabethan audience would not have cared whether he overhears the speech while he is walking towards the speaking character.

In *King Lear*, 2.1, Edmund shouts as if he were fighting with Edgar and calls towards 'within'. Gloucester and his servants do not enter just after the bastard's first call (2.1.31), but do so three and a half lines after Edgar begins to exit (2.1.36). The exit and the entrance are presumably made through different doors. This three-and-a-half-line gap ensures that the entrance of Gloucester and his servants does not overlap with Edgar's exit, though Edgar probably does not need all three and a half lines since he exits running. Neither Edgar's exit nor Gloucester's entrance could be cloaked in darkness, since no stage lighting was used in Elizabethan public playhouses and players acted in broad daylight. Under such stage conditions, the overlapping of the exit and entrance would have seemed inconsistent with the succeeding dialogue. It seems likely, therefore, that the three-and-a-half-line gap reflects Shakespeare's wish to prevent Gloucester's entrance overlapping with Edgar's exit.

There are a great number of instances in Shakespeare's plays where no sooner has a character begun to exit than another character enters. It can be assumed that in such instances the overlapping of exits and entrances is intended or at least permitted. The effects Shakespeare sometimes achieves by overlapping exits and entrances are worth studying.

In *The Merry Wives of Windsor*, 3.3, at the moment the servants begin to exit Ford enters with others, probably through the door towards which the burdened servants are making their exit (3.3.142). The servants cannot walk quickly, because they are carrying the basket in which the fat knight, Falstaff, is hiding. After speaking two and a bit lines while walking towards front-stage, Ford interrupts the servants' move and questions them about the move itself: 'How now? Whether beare you this?' (3.3.146). Watching the basket and Ford, the audience could well imagine the poor knight holding his breath and shrinking under the dirty linen, wishing that the servants would move more quickly and praying that Ford would not search the basket. The humour of the situation, which the audience shares with Mistress Ford and Mistress Page, is clearly based on this image of Falstaff created in the audience's mind, something developing out of the overlap.

In *Antony and Cleopatra*, 1.2, although Cleopatra has been seeking Antony, she impulsively begins to exit the moment she recognizes his entrance (1.2.81), taking her train with her. On the other hand, Antony, who in only the previous scene made the forthright pronouncement, 'Let Rome in Tyber melt' (1.1.35), walks towards front-stage, listening attentively to the messenger from Rome, and does not even perceive the Egyptian party leaving. Rome is everything to Antony now, and Cleopatra instinctively feels it would be vain to compete with Rome.

The Q2 version of *Hamlet* provides another example. In 4.4, while marching in with his army, Fortinbras stops to dispatch a captain to the King of Denmark, and orders the rest of the army to march onwards. The captain would go back towards the door from which he has entered, while Fortinbras and the rest of the army would go on towards the other door. Then Hamlet enters through the door towards which the captain is going. He interrupts the captain's exit and questions him about the exit which Fortinbras and his army are now making. In this way Shakespeare makes Hamlet see Fortinbras only from a distance. This encounter is highly significant, because in the final moments of the tragedy the dying Hamlet gives his vote for Fortinbras and entrusts the future of Denmark to him. However, it is omitted from the F1 text, which was printed from a transcript of the playbook reflecting Shakespeare's revision. It seems that Shakespeare eventually chose to allow only the audience, and not Hamlet, to meet Fortinbras at this stage.[23] Still, it is interesting that Shakespeare did originally intend Hamlet to see Fortinbras by overlapping Hamlet's entrance with Fortinbras's exit, for in both versions they are destined not to meet each other. At the end of the play, a 'warlike noise/noyse' (5.2.301) from Fortinbras's army and Hamlet's 'dying voyce' (5.2.308) merely overlap, and Fortinbras's entrance is too late to be received by Hamlet. If, as suggested above,

Fortinbras in Act 4 appears on stage in armour with his general's truncheon, like the ghost on his first appearances, the F1 change so that Hamlet never sees him has its own potency.[24]

In *Hamlet*, 3.1, Claudius and Polonius exit when Hamlet is approaching. It is not absolutely certain that their departure and Hamlet's arrival are intended to overlap, for Polonius seems to have perceived the approach only aurally ('I heare him comming, let's withdraw my Lord' (3.1.57)), and Hamlet neither speaks to them nor refers to their exit. Hamlet may possibly enter after the King and Polonius complete their exit. But Ophelia, who is on stage, speaks no lines to fill the gap. If Hamlet enters by one door while the King and Polonius are exiting towards the other door or the central hangings,[25] the overlapping of the exit of the King and Polonius and the entrance of Hamlet adds to the suspense. The audience must suspect that Hamlet may be aware of the King and Polonius, for Hamlet and the King have been trying to conceal their own real intentions and probe each other's heart.

The overlapping of exits and entrances is not always so obviously meaningful. Their effect is often very subtle. But, however vague the result of an overlapping exit and entrance may seem, if it was an element in the experience of Shakespeare's original audience we should not ignore it.

A break between Shakespearian scenes generally begins with the exit of all characters, and the new scene opens with the entrance of other characters. It is reasonable to assume that the closing exit of one scene and the opening entrance of the next are made through different doors. Variations on this pattern might, however, occur where the exit at the end of one scene and the next scene's entrance overlap.

Bernard Beckerman argues that the overlapping of exits and entrances was not a habit of the Globe company and that separation and pause was the more likely method.[26] The occurrence of split exits and entrances is a sufficient reason for suggesting that exits to close one scene and entrances to open another did not always overlap, because where the same door is used for both the exit and the entrance, the entrance cannot be made until the exit is completed. We agree with Beckerman when he suggests that characters took several paces towards the centre or front of the stage before speaking at the beginnings of scenes, and that this action may have provided a hiatus sufficient to mark a new scene.[27] It is certain that there must have been a pause between the concluding speech of one scene and the opening speech of the next. However, scenes change very frequently in Shakespeare's plays. Act 4 of *Antony and Cleopatra* has sixteen scenes. There are many scenes which run for only ten or so lines. It seems unlikely that since it took four lines for characters to complete their exit, and a further two to four lines for other characters to walk towards the centre or front of the stage, there must have been a six-to-eight-line pause at every scene-break.

Surviving theatre manuscripts are a help. In the extant manuscript of Thomas Heywood's *The Captives*, the book-keeper regularly places the word 'clere' at the ends of scenes.[28] This is weighty evidence for scene-breaks, even taking into account the fact that it comes from the Cockpit company, not the Globe. However, did the book-keeper insert the word to indicate that the enterers should not appear until the exiters had completely disappeared from the stage? The following passage is from John Marston's *Antonio and Mellida*, a Paul's Children's play:

> *Feli.* Peace, here comes the Prologue, cleare the Stage.
> > *Exeunt.*
> > *The Prologue.*
> THE wreath of pleasure, and delicious sweetes,
>
> > (lines 153–7)[29]

Feliche's last speech referring to the Prologue's entrance serves as a bridge between the Induction and the Prologue. The exit of Feliche and others and the entrance of the Prologue overlap. Since, in this instance, 'cleare the Stage' means 'let us all leave the stage', it may be that the Cockpit book-keeper also used 'clere' only to indicate that all the on-stage characters should exit.

There are similar instances in *Measure for Measure* and *Cymbeline*, when Claudio is first brought in by the Provost (*Measure*, 1.2.104–7), and when the gentlemen herald the entry of Posthumus and Imogen with the Queen (*Cymbeline*, 1.1.69–70). In each case, despite the fact that F1 marks a scene division, most editors continue the scene. However, if there really is a scene change where F1 indicates one, it shows an overlapping exit and entrance at the scene-break. On the other hand, if the scene divisions are merely scribal in origin and have nothing to do with theatrical practice (both of the F1 texts of *Measure* and *Cymbeline* were printed from literary transcripts by Ralph Crane),[30] then in each case Shakespeare continues the scene by over-lapping the exit and the entrance.

At the end of *Romeo and Juliet*, 1.4, Romeo and his friends do not leave the stage altogether but only move aside. According to Q2, *They march about the Stage, and Servingmen come forth with Napkins.* This stage direction clearly indicates that the end of 1.4 flows into the opening of 1.5. In *A Midsummer Night's Dream* at the end of Act 3 the lovers do not exit but remain on stage asleep. Since one scene often flows into the next, it is not unreasonable to conclude that the original staging allowed exits and entrances to overlap at scene-breaks.

While act-breaks almost invariably emptied the stage in Shake-speare's plays, and the same characters who exit almost never re-enter, there are a great number of instances in which a character exits at or around the end of a scene and enters at or around the beginning of the succeeding scene. If scene-breaks did not provide the time necessary for the actors to complete their exits and also move across off-stage to the opposite door, the necessary time had to be built into the dialogue. Where a character appears in two consecutive scenes, the number of lines between the point at which he begins his exit and his re-entry is revealing. To identify the time allowed for these instances, we have checked all the cases in the early printed texts, using only entrances and exits on the main stage, as before.

The instances can be divided into the following six kinds, according to the conditions found between the exits and the entrances, mainly at the ends of the preceding scenes or at the beginnings of the succeeding scenes. They fall into these distinct categories:

1. Excursion   An excursion, military marching, or the like.
2. Action   A different kind of action.
3. Last   A character enters last after several other characters have entered.[31]
4. Sound   An off-stage sound or music.
5. Split   The closing exit or the opening entrance may be split.
6. None   A situation involving none of the above five con-ditions.

Table 2. Instances fulfilling each condition

Condition	Number of lines										
	0	1	2	3	4	5	6	7	8	9	10
Excursion	17	0	0	1	1	0	1	0	1	0	0
Action	3	0	0	0	0	0	0	2	0	0	0
Last	5	0	0	0	0	0	0	0	0	0	0
Sound	11	0	1	0	4	0	2	0	1	2	3
Split	0	1	0	0	0	1	0	1	0	1	2
None	5	0	0	1	2	3	7	6	4	12	4

Notes:
    ^ In this table, extra part-lines are counted as full lines.
    ᴮ Wherever an instance fulfils two or more of these conditions, we have included it with the first.
    ᶜ When characters who have exited at the same time enter at different times, or vice versa, we have used the smallest line number.

Needless to say, it is only the last category that reveals how many lines are allowed for characters to exit and walk to the opposite door. But it is also important to grasp the difference between the distribution of instances fulfilling any of the first five conditions and that of instances of 'None'. It is sufficient for the present purposes to show the number of instances fulfilling each condition in which the number of lines is between nought and ten.

While there are numerous instances fulfilling any of the five conditions (1–5) in which the number of lines is zero, there are only a few instances of 'None' in which the number is below six.[32] Furthermore, *The Tempest*, 4.1.264–5.1.0 (Prospero, Ariel) and possibly *Titus Andronicus*, 3.2.84–4.1.0 (Young Lucius, Lavinia) need not be counted as instances of 'None' with no lines, because the Blackfriars, for which *The Tempest* was written, used act-breaks, and Young Lucius and Lavinia's immediate re-entrance, which occurs only in the F1 text, appears to reflect later staging after the practice of act-breaks was adopted by the King's Men (*c.* 1607–10).[33] Some instances require the actor to change costumes off-stage between his exit and re-entry. But where none of the five conditions is fulfilled, the number of lines is never fewer than sixteen.[34] Since in Shakespeare's plays characters are usually allowed about four lines to walk from front-stage to a stage door, it can be concluded that in almost all the cases where no action is made or no sound is heard, a sufficient number of lines are spoken to fill not only the time for the characters to complete their exits but also at least part of the necessary time for them to move across off-stage to the opposite door.[35]

It may have been usual, at least at the Theatre and the Globe, for actors to enter and open a new scene while other actors were still making their exit at the end of the previous scene, except where both stage doors were simultaneously used for the closing exit or the opening entrance. This may not apply to the staging at the Rose and the Blackfriars, because of their smaller stages.

At the end of 3.2 of *Richard II*, written for the Theatre, Richard departs with his friends after saying:

> He does me double wrong,
> That wounds me with the flatteries of his tong,
> Discharge my followers, let them hence away,
> From Richards night, to Bullingbrookes faire day.

(3.2.211–4)

The next scene, 3.3, begins with the arrival of Bullingbrook and his followers. The overlapping of the exit of a character who has sunk into the depths of despair with the entrance of the one who has driven him to that despair would stress the contrast between the falling fortunes of Richard and the rising fortunes of Bullingbrook, and make the exit of Richard and his friends more miserable and the entrance of Bullingbrook and his followers more powerful. In this way, at the Theatre and the Globe, the overlapping of the closing exit of one scene and the opening entrance of the next could make the juxtaposition of the two scenes obvious and intensify the effect of the juxtaposition itself.

The Three Openings
in the frons

a. The Use of the Flanking Doors

It is generally agreed that Shakespeare's playhouses had three entry-ways in the *frons*, i.e. two flanking doors and a central doorway or aperture. The bald direction '*Enter*' or '*Exit/Exeunt*' ignores this multiple resource, and any conceptualization of the early staging must identify which of the various openings the players would normally expect to use. The flanking doors were the standard means of entry for most of the characters, and the ways these entry-points were used need to be considered first.

A break between Shakespearian scenes generally begins with the departure of all characters, and the new scene opens with the entrance of other characters. What we will call Postulate A here assumes that the closing exit of a scene and the opening entrance of the next scene are usually made through different doors. Even if the closing exit of one scene and the opening entrance of the next do not overlap, it is certain that the enterers had to be in position behind the opposite door to that used by the exiters, before they complete their exit. If the enterers failed to do so, the scene changes would not flow smoothly.

In Shakespeare's plays there are very many instances where a character has just begun to exit when another character enters. The exit ends the flow of dialogue which has been going on and the entrance of the other character begins a new flow of dialogue. It is reasonable to suppose that the two characters would use different doors, because they do not usually exchange speeches. In the cases of simultaneous or overlapping exits and entrances, it is essential to the smooth flow of the action that the exiter and enterer use different doors (this we call Postulate B). Postulate B implies that before the exiter begins to leave, the enterer has to be ready behind the opposite door.

Whether at scene breaks or within scenes, the frequency of overlapping and juxtaposition for exits and entrances seems, indirectly but strongly, to confirm Bernard Beckerman's view that there was some convention which governed the use of the stage doors. He points out that the extant Elizabethan theatrical plots indicate entrances without identifying which door is to be used, and conjectures that 'entrances were made at one conventionally designated door and exits at the other unless the actor was specifically instructed otherwise'.[1] This theory takes account of Postulates A and B, and it can solve the practical problems these postulates entail, such as whether the enterers could easily decide which door they had to stand ready to use. This simple rule would have been of particularly practical value to minor actors doubling several roles.

It is therefore helpful to adopt Beckerman's hypothesis (which might be called the 'O' rule), at least tentatively, as a general principle concerning entrances and exits on the Shakespearian stage. One door was normally used for entrances, and the other for exits. However, several patterns of entrances and exits violate this general principle. If we assume that normally one of the flanking doors served as the 'entrance door' and the other as the 'exit door', some modifications to the rule must have existed. The following are patterns in which either enterers had to use the 'exit door' or exiters used the 'entrance door'.

Pattern i. Simultaneous Entrances. Where two enterers meet on the stage, the two doors represent different directions, and one of the two enterers has to use the 'exit door'. The great majority of these cases occur at the beginnings of scenes. Most entry stage directions including *'severally'*, *'at several doors'*, *'at one door . . . at another [at the other]'* and the like are opening stage directions. Where one enterer greets the other at the opening of a scene, and where one asks the other who he is, where he is going, or where he has come from, even if the opening stage direction does not explicitly indicate the use of different doors it is most likely that the two enterers make a simultaneous entrance by the opposing doors.

However, it may not always be the case that two enterers had to use different doors simply because such a greeting or question is offered at the beginning of a scene. For one thing, it is possible that such speeches are meant only to imply that the enterers met just before their appearance. For another, in a few cases the enterers may be intended to enter one after the other from the same door. The opening stage direction of Barnabe Barnes's *The Devil's Charter*, 1.3 reads '*Enter* Gismond di Visselli, *and after him* Barbarossa.'[2] Although Barbarossa asks Gismond where he is going, and Gismond is pleased to have encountered Barbarossa, they do not make a simultaneous entrance, and therefore must use the same door. The use of the same door for successive entrances was clearly more desirable for fluent scene changes. The opening stage direction of *Julius Caesar*, 1.3 reads '*Thunder, and Lightning. Enter Caska, and Cicero.*' The comma between '*Caska*' and '*and*' may be significant, for it is possibly an indication that Caska and Cicero enter separately from the same door. Although the entry stage direction mentions Caska first, Cicero speaks first. If Caska enters first, he could make a gesture of amazement to fill the time before Cicero enters and addresses him.

Pattern ii. Simultaneous Exits. When two characters separate to depart in different directions, one or the other must exit from the 'entrance door'. In these cases, whichever character is nearer to the 'entrance door' would automatically go towards it, and the character nearer to the 'exit door' would naturally go out through it. There are very few exit stage directions in the Quarto and Folio texts of Shakespeare's plays explicitly indicating that the exiters should use different doors. This paucity might suggest that the characters who bid farewell to each other were expected to depart through opposing doors.

However, there are many instances where two characters bid farewell to each other at the end of a scene, and in some of them the two characters do not need to exit from different doors. At the end of *The Merchant of Venice*, 3.1, for example, Shylock and Tubal do not have to exit from different doors, for Shylock's speech does not necessarily imply that they start moving in opposite directions.

> *Shy.* Nay, that's true, that's very true, goe *Tuball* see me an
> Officer, bespeake him a fortnight before, I will have the
> hart of him if he forfeite, for were he out of Venice I

can make what merchandize I will: goe *Tuball*, and
meete me at our Sinagogue, goe good *Tuball*, at our
Sinagogue *Tuball*.

Exeunt.

(3.1.116–21)

It is certainly possible in some instances for two exiters to go together
towards the same door just after or while bidding farewell to each
other.

As John Orrell has observed, Shakespeare usually arranges the ends
of scenes in such a way that the closing exits do not cause any delay to
the opening entrances of the succeeding scenes.[3] For example, *1 Henry
VI*, 1.1 and *Hamlet*, 1.2 begin with processions, but end with solo exits.
Alan C. Dessen suggests that in certain instances, despite the stage
direction '*Exeunt (omnes)*', the exiters are likely to leave separately, a
few lines apart.[4] This may be applicable to the example from *The
Merchant*; it is possible that Tubal starts to go, stops, and restarts while
Shylock is speaking and that Shylock does not begin to exit until he
finishes speaking. Given the size of the early stages, many instances of
apparently simultaneous exits may have been either joint departures or
successive exits.

*Pattern iii. Entrances and Exits of Two Opposing Characters or
Groups.* We can conclude from these examples that when two opposing characters or groups made entrances or exits simultaneously or
successively they normally used different doors. Such symmetrical
entrances or exits would emphasize the opposition between the
two characters or groups. In *A Midsummer Night's Dream*, 2.1, the
stage direction for Oberon and Titania's first entrance explicitly indicates that they use different doors: '*Enter the King of Fairies, at one
doore, with his traine; and the Queene, at another, with hers*' (2.1.59).
Their difference and division are symbolically shown by their split
entrance.

'*Excursions*' involve the entrance and exit of two armies. Some
Elizabethan stage directions concerning excursions indicate pursuits.

Alarum within: Excursions over thee Stage.
The Lackies running, Maillard following them.

(Chapman, *The Revenge of Bussy D'Ambois* Q1, G1r)[5]

Excursions. The Bastard pursues *Austria*, and kills him.

(Anon., *1 The Troublesome Reign of King John* Q1, E2r)[6]

It appears to have been the custom that, in excursions, instead of a confrontation, one army pursued the other, both entering from one door, making a great sweep over the stage, and exiting by the other door.

Pattern iv: Entering Character Meets Exiting Character. In Chettle, Dekker, and Haughton's *Patient Grissil*, 2.2, as Grissil exits, Mario and Lepido '*Enter at the same doore*' (2.2.122).[7] The dialogue requires the exiter and the enterers to pass each other. There are some other stage directions which indicate that an entering character meets an exiting character: e.g., '*Enter Dalavill meeting Young Garaldine going out*' (Heywood, *The English Traveller*, Act 5);[8] '*Enter Clem meeting Joffer*' (Heywood, *The Fair Maid of the West, Part II*, Act 1).[9] In these cases it is almost certain that the enterer and the exiter use the same door. On the other hand, Shakespeare's plays provide no instances where an entering character and an exiting character must use the same door. Possibly, in those cases where an enterer and an exiter exchange words, they are intended to use the same door.[10]

Pattern v. Entrance and Immediate Exit. Where a character enters and immediately exits, unless the dialogue implies the character's move across the stage, it may be more natural for him to exit from the door through which he has just entered. There are quite a few instances where characters are brought on stage only to be told to leave immediately.[11] In these cases, the characters would stop near their entry door during their very short presence on stage, and exit through the same door.

Pattern vi. Exit and Immediate Re-entrance. Contrariwise, when a character absents himself from the stage for a very short time, unless his off-stage move is implied in the dialogue his exit and re-entrance have to be made through the same door. Towards the end of *Richard III*, 1.4, when the First Murderer carries Clarence's body away and returns immediately to tell the Second Murderer to stop shirking and help him, it is natural for him to re-enter through the door from which he has exited. Indeed he cannot avoid using the same door, for there are only three lines between the point at which he begins to exit (1.4.265) and the point at which he enters again (1.4.268), and three lines do not provide enough time for an actor to complete an exit and also cross off-stage to the opposite door. When the First Murderer exits, he does not foretell his immediate re-entrance, which is caused by the Second Murderer's delay. In such an instance, it is very natural for the exiter to make his exit and then re-enter and exit again from the 'exit door'.[12]

Pattern vii. Exiting to Fetch Something and Re-enter with It. There are instances in which a character exits to fetch something and re-enters with it, or exits to obtain information and re-enters with it. In most such cases, the exit itself leads to the expectation that its related re-entrance will be made through the same door. Instances where a newcomer's arrival is announced in advance by a character who has investigated an off-stage sound are quite common. There are also many instances in which a servant is summoned by his master, and ordered to bring something. In these instances, the servant enters, immediately exits and almost as quickly re-enters. In *Julius Caesar*, 2.1, for example, Lucius must repeat the action of this pattern several times. This pattern is very often expanded to include an additional earlier or later entrance. Where a character exits to pursue some off-stage business he normally uses the 'entrance door', behind which the necessary property is ready.

In *A Midsummer Night's Dream*, 2.1, however, Puck exits to fetch the magic flower for Oberon at line 176, but does not re-enter until line 246. During his relatively long absence, Demetrius and Helena's arrival and departure take place. As the dialogue suggests, Puck's exit is a long-distance journey as well as a temporary absence: Puck's speech before the exit is 'Ile put a girdle, round about the earth, in forty minutes' (2.1.175–6). It may be that for this event he exits from the 'exit door' and returns through the 'entrance door', for whether Puck returns from the same door after such a long interim may be a matter not needing the kind of consistency that briefer gaps between exit and re-entry demand. Moreover, an off-stage crossing might contribute to the impression that he has made a long-distance journey.

Pattern viii. Summoner's Exit and Summoned Character's Entrance. Where a character exits to summon another character and the summoned character enters either alone or with the summoner, the summoned character would naturally enter through the door from which the summoner has exited. As with pattern vii, this pattern is very often related to an additional earlier entrance; there are many instances in which a character enters only to announce that another character is waiting off stage and exits to return with him immediately. In pattern viii, the exit is no more than a subordinate move to the entrance. It is most likely that in such cases the summoner generally exits by the 'entrance door', behind which the summoned character waits.

In *The Taming of the Shrew*, 5.2, Biondello's two exits and re-entrances as a messenger to Bianca and the Widow, Grumio's exit to summon Katherine and her entrance, and Katherine's exit to summon the other wives and her re-entrance with them are presumably all made through the same door. However, whether this door should be the same one from which the three wives exited earlier in this scene is not certain, because there is a 33-line gap between their exit (5.2.50) and Biondello's first exit (5.2.83). In *The Tempest*, 5.1, Ariel exits to fetch the Ship-master and Boatswain at line 105, and returns with them at line 218. This example is very similar to Puck's exit to fetch the magic flower. For the same reasons, in *The Tempest*, 5.1, Ariel might depart by the 'exit door' and re-enter with the mariners from the 'entrance door'.

Pattern ix. Summoner's Entrance and Summoned Character's Exit. Where a character enters to summon an on-stage character to go off, and they exit together, it is natural that they should exit through the door from which the summoner has entered.[13] From the fact that in such instances the entrance is nothing more than a preparatory move made for the exit, and that the majority of these instances occur at the ends of scenes, it seems very likely that in this pattern the summoners enter through the 'exit door'. If they do, the opening entrances of the succeeding scenes can be made from the 'entrance door', in accordance with Postulate A set out at the beginning of this chapter.

Pattern x: Entrance and Exit by a Door Representing the Entrance to a Particular Place. Among Shakespeare's plays, *The Comedy of Errors* appears to be unique in using the conventionalized arcade setting of academic drama. This play was performed in the 1594 Christmas revels at Gray's Inn. According to T. S. Dorsch, the three inner doors at the west end of the Gray's hall would have served as the entrances to the Phoenix, the Porpentine, and the Priory, and the outer doors could well have been left open to represent the ways leading to the port and the city.[14] Assuming the play was performed in a public playhouse, it is not certain whether the three houses might have been represented by the same doors throughout the performance, for not only the three houses but also the standard entryways had to be represented by the three entries of the tiring-house wall. The doors for entrances and exits in this play are uniquely odd and distinctive. It does seem most likely that each house was represented by the same door at least throughout each scene when the three locations were in use.

In other plays there are instances where a stage door temporarily represents the entrance to a particular place. In such cases the entrances and exits related to the place are made from that door. Conversely, those unrelated to the place cannot be made through such a door until it becomes simply a neutral stage door again. In *Romeo and Juliet*, 5.1, it is absolutely necessary for the Apothecary to appear and leave through the door which Romeo identifies as the entrance of his shop.[15] Needless to say, Romeo cannot use the same door for his exit, even if it is the 'exit door'. It is merely a neutral stage door until Romeo transforms it into 'the entrance of the Apothecary's shop' by saying 'As I remember this should be the house' (5.1.56), probably walking towards the door. His move would be useful to change the location of the scene from 'a street in Mantua' to 'in front of the Apothecary's shop'. In other words, the location of the first half of this scene is ambiguous, while that of the second half is specific.

It is clear that the opening stage direction of *Richard III*, 3.2, '*Enter a Messenger to the Doore of Hastings*', indicates that the messenger enters from one door and crosses the stage to the other. By crossing to and knocking at the other door, he transforms it into 'the Doore of Hastings'. Since most instances of this pattern occur at the openings of scenes, we may assume that the visitor normally enters by the 'entrance door' and the visited character enters from the 'exit door'. In the case of *Richard III*, 3.2, how long does that door remain the entrance to Hastings's house after he has entered from it? If it should remain so throughout the scene, all the succeeding entrances and exits should be made through the door which the messenger has just used.[16] Thereafter in this scene, however, there are three instances of simultaneous or overlapping exits and entrances (3.2.31, 90–1, 103). In each case, bearing in mind Postulate B, it would be very awkward for the exiter(s) and enterer to use the same door. When Lord Hastings addresses an entering pursuivant, saying 'How now, Sirrha? how goes the World with thee?' (3.2.92), the location seems to have already become very ambiguous. The words could be spoken to a passer-by in a street. Not until the 'exit door' and the 'entrance door' are simultaneously used for the messenger's exit and Catesby's entrance (3.2.31), does the 'exit door' completely regain its normal neutrality.

The patterns listed above are by no means fixed; indeed, the evidence can usually bear two different interpretations. Since there are so many cases of violation, we could conclude that Beckerman's proposition that entrances are usually made by one flanking door and exits are normally made by the other would not have worked as the players' standard practice. We would have to look for another principle.[7] But are these patterns too complicated to have been used as their routine rule of thumb by Shakespearian players? They are based on no more than three main modes of practice. There are simultaneous moves in different directions (patterns i–iv); moves making up a continuous action (patterns v–ix); and moves related to a particular place (pattern x). The players could have inferred which rule they should follow instinctively from the dialogue. This means that Beckerman's general principle would have worked well, even if detailed rules or patterns had not been expressly formulated or rehearsed. Even in the instances where the same door is used for the entrance and the exit, the idea of one being the 'entrance door' and the other the 'exit door' is helpful for the actors to decide which door to use. Beckerman's hypothesis that in Elizabethan playhouses one stage door was conventionally designated as the 'entrance door' while the other was regularly designated as the 'exit door' may have been the players' rule of thumb.

b. The Use of the Central Opening

In the early texts of Shakespearian and non-Shakespearian plays, if we exclude stage directions for discoveries we find relatively few entry and exit stage directions that explicitly indicate the use of the central opening. Most of the examples we have are for triple entrances and exits, such as '*Enter severall wayes, Bastard, Alanson, Reignier, halfe ready, and halfe unready*' (*1 Henry VI*, 2.1.39); '*Exeunt severally*' (*The*

Two Noble Kinsmen, 1.5.16), which is for the three queens who have entered with the hearses of their husbands; and '*Enter* Urcenze *and* Onophrio *at severall doores, and* Farnezie *in the mid'st*' (*Patient Grissil*, 3.2.0). However, in addition to 'discoveries' and triple entrances and exits, several other kinds of situation might have benefited from the use of the central opening.

Cave Scenes. Let us begin with relatively secure instances. There are stage directions reading '*Enter Timon from his Cave*' (*Timon of Athens*, 5.1.29); '*Enter Timon out of his Cave*' (*Timon of Athens*, 5.2.15); and '*Enter Belarius, Guiderius, Arviragus, and Imogen from the Cave*' (*Cymbeline*, 4.2.0). It is more likely than not that in these cases the enterers appear from the central opening, because this special entryway would most fittingly represent the entrance to a recessed place, such as a cave. The largest opening in the *frons* is a better choice of entry-point for such events than the only obvious alternative, the stage trap. After he has discarded human society, Timon might possibly make all his entrances and exits by the central opening. When a soldier seeks Timon in 5.4, the soldier would naturally direct his speech towards the central opening, and he might discover Timon's tomb, possibly by drawing back the hangings.[18]

In *King Lear*, 3.4, the central opening may well represent the 'hovel' of Poor Tom, into which the Fool goes, and out of which he comes almost immediately. In *The Tempest*, 5.1, Prospero '*discovers Ferdinand and Miranda, playing at Chesse*' (5.1.173), saying, 'This Cell's my Court:...pray you looke in' (5.1.168–9). Clearly, in this scene, the central opening serves as Prospero's cell. Some time later, towards the end of the play, Prospero first tells Caliban to take Stefano and Trinculo to his cell (5.1.295–6), and then invites Alonso and his train there (5.1.304–5). We can reasonably be sure that the central opening was used in *The Tempest* for the final exits of Caliban and his companions, Prospero's guests and Ferdinand and Miranda, and Prospero himself.

In *A Midsummer Night's Dream*, Titania falls asleep in 2.2 and awakes in 3.1. Stanley Wells notes that it is not necessary for her to be visible to the audience all this time. He suggests the possibility that 'on the Elizabethan stage she occupied a recess that could be curtained off at the end of Oberon's spell'.[19] At the beginning of 3.1, when

Quince suggests to his fellow mechanicals that they use the 'hauthorne brake' as their 'tyring house' (3.1.4), he would point to one of the three openings in the *frons*. The 'brake' may have been represented by the hangings concealing the central opening. Bottom retires into the 'tyring house' and returns with an ass head on. The transformed Bottom's re-entrance through the curtains would be the most impressive way of exhibiting him in his new guise. This would gain extra resonance if Titania had been there previously.

Hiding behind the Hangings. When an on-stage character hides behind the hangings, it seems sometimes to have been treated as an exit by Shakespeare, the book-keeper, and their fellow actors. *1 Henry IV* F1 marks an exit at the point where Falstaff hides behind the arras (2.5.510), whereas Q1 supplies no exit. It may be that the exit stage direction was added to F1 to indicate the departure of other thieves, because Falstaff does not leave the stage altogether. But *Hamlet* Q1 gives an exit stage direction for Corambis's action of going behind the arras in 3.4. Although neither Q2 nor F1 *Hamlet* provides any stage direction for Polonius's hiding in this scene, it is certain that at least the Q1 actor-reporter regarded Polonius's (Corambis's) action as an exit. In Beaumont and Fletcher's *Philaster*, a play of the King's Men, Gallatea hides to overhear the conversation between Pharamond and Megra, and later reappears. The Q2 text of this play gives the following exit and entry stage directions for her actions: '*Exit* Gall *behind the hangings*' (2.2.52); '*Enter* Gallatea *from behind the hangings*' (2.2.133).[20] This raises the important question whether the three doorways were all routinely curtained off, or whether the flanking doors were normally free of curtaining. Most likely, in those scenes where an on-stage character hides behind the arras in order to avoid meeting someone entering from one of the flanking doors, neither the door used by the enterer nor the one opposite was curtained off, but only the central opening had hangings. When they hide the 'exiters' go behind the hangings concealing the central doorway.

    If hiding behind the arras was sometimes treated as an exit, it is necessary to reconsider *Hamlet*, 3.1 and 3.4. In 3.1, Polonius and the King have scarcely perceived Hamlet's approach when they withdraw. The F1 text provides an exit stage direction for their movement. However, Polonius's plan was that the King and he hide 'behinde an

Arras' (2.2.164) and eavesdrop on Hamlet's conversation with Ophelia. It is therefore possible that they *'exit behind the arras'*, instead of departing through a side door.[21] Either way, they are absent from the stage during Hamlet's conversation with Ophelia, but the two ways of exiting differ in the extent to which the audience is conscious of the presence of the eavesdroppers. If they hide behind the arras, the suspense the audience experiences during the dialogue between Hamlet and Ophelia would be much keener, especially when Hamlet abruptly asks Ophelia, 'Where's your Father?' (3.1.132), and aggressively says, 'Those that are married already, all but one shall live' (3.1.150–1). In 3.4, Hamlet certainly stabs Polonius to death through the arras covering the central opening. If this is the second time of his *'exiting behind the arras'*, the first time with Claudius, and Hamlet knew they were there, the audience might think Hamlet's violent action the second time a little more understandable.

Siege Scenes. In Elizabethan plays, siege scenes where defenders appear above on the 'walls' to parley with besiegers standing below before the 'gates' are common. Shakespeare uses several such scenes. Although it is not certain whether the 'gates' were always represented by the central opening, clearly the use of the central opening would have brought about some effect that could not have been expected from the use of a flanking door. *King John*, 2.1 takes place before the gates of Angiers. The Kings of France and England separately demand that the gates be open to them, but neither is admitted. The two opposing groups, i.e. the French–Austrian and the English armies, exit from different doors, and after excursions, they enter again from different doors.[22] Their ways of entering and exiting suggest that the central opening was used as the gates of the town. The two kings accept the citizen's suggestion about the conjunction between the Dauphin and Lady Blanche so that they can be admitted to the town. When the two armies finally march in through the gates, after making their entrances and exits by the different side doors, this joint departure through the central opening would become the symbol of the peace now established between England and France, though the Bastard's delayed exit reveals the fragile quality of the truce.

Evidently, the highlight of a siege scene is the moment when the besieged characters descend from the 'walls' and open the 'gates' to the besiegers. The defenders' descent from the upper playing level and their appearance through the finally opened central opening symbolically express their formal, unconditional surrender. By contrast, the besiegers' march off through the central opening visibly shows their triumph. In the Flint Castle scene of *Richard II*, Richard comes down from the balcony to the 'base court' (3.3.175, 179, 181). There is no mention of gates in this scene. Whether Richard appears on the stage below the balcony from the central opening or from a flanking door is a decisive factor in the visual effect of his descent. In Shakespeare's playhouses, there were no external stairs between the upper playing level and the main stage, and so only the beginning and completion of the descent were visible. Using the central opening for Richard's arrival on stage would give an exact symbolic form to his downfall and surrender.

When in *Henry V* Henry besieges Harfleur, according to the F1 stage direction, he enters the stage with '*all his Traine before the Gates*' (3.3.83). Although the Chorus repeatedly refers to the poor condition of the English army and requests the audience to use their imagination, the army is, at this point, intended to look as powerful as possible. Presenting the English army on stage would have used all the available players, who would have followed Henry by marching off at the end through the central opening representing the town gates.

Masques, Shows, and Ghost Scenes. There is a strong likelihood that a cave and the like were represented by the central opening. It is therefore noteworthy that some masques and shows in the plays involved a cave or something similar. This is one such case:

> *Dumb shew. A cave suddenly breakes open, and out of it comes* Falshood, (*attir'd as* Truth *is*) *her face spotted, shee stickes up her banner on the top of the Cave*; ...
>
> (Dekker, *The Whore of Babylon*, 4.1.0)[23]

The two versions of *The Battle of Alcazar*, its printed text and its 'plot', have particular interest as evidence for its original staging. If, as David Bradley concludes, the Quarto text represents with reasonable accuracy the copy as it left Peele's hands,[24] it can be inferred from a comparison between the Q text and the plot that it was the bookkeeper who decided that the three Furies should lie 'behind the Curtaines ... one wth a whipp: a nother wth a blody torch: & the 3ᵈ wth a Chopping knife' in the dumb show presented during the second chorus.²⁵ According to the Presenter's description of the Furies in the Q text, 'they lie, | In cave as darke as hell, and beds of steele' (lines 324– 5). Since the book-keeper bothered to provide annotations for their properties, they would have actually shown their fearful appearances from behind the hangings, 'Alecto with her brand and bloudie torch, | Megaera with her whip and snakie haire, | Tisiphone with her fatall murthering yron' (lines 334–6). Where the entrance or exit itself is meant to be spectacular, the case for the use of the central opening is a strong one.²⁶

In the last scene of *As You Like It*, Hymen enters with Rosalind and Celia. The god presents Rosalind to Duke Senior, saying, '*Good Duke receive thy daughter,* | *Hymen from Heaven brought her,...*' (5.4.109–10). Although the Globe may have been furnished with a descent machine from the start,²⁷ Shakespeare did not make this god fly. Since Rosalind has previously said that she is a 'Magitian' (5.2.68), possibly the audience should understand that a lord is playing Hymen at Rosalind's request. The text itself provides nothing to suggest that Hymen is anything other than a god. On either view of the matter it is unlikely that such a magical figure would make an entrance from one of the flanking doors. The central opening is more appropriate for this special entrance made by the god of marriage accompanied by the two brides. They might even be 'discovered' and come out towards the other characters on stage.

In *Antonio's Revenge* Q₁ there is a stage direction reading '*Maria draweth the courtaine: and the ghost of Andrugio is displayed, sitting on the bed*' (lines 1280–1).²⁸ Whether the curtain is a bed curtain or a stage curtain depends on whether the bed was pushed out onto the main stage or merely 'discovered'.²⁹ This example may suggest the possibility that ghosts as well as deities sometimes entered through the hangings. In *Hamlet*, 3.4, the ghost of Hamlet's father makes his last appearance. The Q₁ text clearly indicates that the ghost enters '*in his night gowne*' and Hamlet declares that he exits by the 'Portall' (3.4.127). In addition to his domestic costume, his arrival and departure by the entryway which can be associated with Gertrude's bed chamber would emphasize his intimacy with her. The central opening seems most appropriate in this scene for the entrance and exit of the ghost who was once a loving husband.³⁰

Choruses are different from other characters in that they speak from outside the play. They generally appear on the stage at special moments, the opening of the play, between acts, and at the end. It is likely that these figures also use the central opening for their entrances and exits, unless there is a particular reason why they cannot use it.[31] In the Prologue to *Romeo and Juliet*, the Chorus delivers a conventional, formal speech which is written in the form of a sonnet. After the Chorus's departure, the characters belonging to the '*Two households both alike in dignitie*' (Pro. 1) enter successively from opposing side doors. In the Choruses of scenes 5, 10, and 18 of *Pericles*, Gower introduces and explains dumb shows, in which two groups of characters enter from different stage doors, make gestures, and depart from different doors. In *The Winter's Tale* Time, the Chorus, presumably a bald old man with wings and an hour glass,[32] enters to bridge the sixteen-year gap between the tragic and comic halves of the play. It is particularly tempting to speculate that these figures all use the central opening for their entrances and exits. Such entrances and exits would contribute to the formality and symmetry of their scenes.

Further uses of the central opening are in *Love's Labour's Lost*, 5.2, *A Midsummer Night's Dream*, 5.1, and *Hamlet*, 3.2, which all provide an example of a play within the play. It is likely that the actors performing the play within the play used the central opening for their entrances and exits. If this was the case, the stage audiences for these performances would have sat at front-stage, facing the central opening.[33]

Ceremonial Processions. It would seem appropriate for certain royal ceremonial processions to be made from the central opening. This does not apply to processions passing across the stage, e.g. the procession in *Julius Caesar*, 1.2, or the coronation procession in *Henry VIII*, 4.1. Examples of royal processions using the central opening are the scenes which would require the chair of state. In *Richard II*, 1.1 and 1.3, *Hamlet*, 1.2, and *King Lear*, 1.1, the kings are likely to make their ceremonial entrances through the central opening preceded by stage hands who position the dais and canopy, before they take their royal chairs. The spectacular entrances they make are a manifestation of their power and authority, which Richard and Lear are to lose shortly, and which Claudius has recently acquired because of the death of the king whose ghost appeared in the previous scene.

Some histories and most tragedies end with funeral processions. These processions might also have made their exits through the central opening. If, for example, Richard II's coffin and the dead bodies of Hamlet and Lear are carried away through the central opening, Richard and Lear would symbolically re-acquire, by this act, the royal status which they had earlier lost, and in Hamlet's case it would be visual confirmation of Fortinbras's words that 'had he beene put on | [Hamlet would] have prov'd most royally' (5.2.351–2). The Q2 and F1 texts of *Hamlet* differ about the number of bodies Fortinbras orders his soldiers to carry away at the end of the play. The difference may possibly imply that, for practical reasons, Shakespeare finally ought to have allowed the dead bodies of Claudius, Gertrude, and Laertes to stand up and leave the stage after the end of the play. When the dead body of Hamlet was treated with regal dignity, the contrast of leaving the dead body of Claudius on the stage would have been even more effective.³⁴

In *The Tempest*, after the opening storm scene, Prospero enters with Miranda. To judge from the fact that he later tells her to 'Lend [her] hand | And plucke [his] Magick garment from [him]' (1.2.23–4), he enters in his magic cloak, and presumably with a magic staff. The central opening, rather than one of the flanking doors, may be appropriate for the entrance which the ruler of the island first makes just after he has used his magic. However, later in the same scene, when Prospero summons Caliban, from which entryway does the servant make his first appearance? Caliban enters just after Ariel exits from one of the side doors. If Caliban appears from the opposite side door, the visual contrast between the airy spirit and the earthy monster would be symmetrically intensified. But Caliban's complaint about being kept 'In this hard Rocke' (1.2.346) seems to suggest the entry-point which is fitter to represent a recessed place, i.e. either the central opening³⁵ or the trap. The central opening is likelier than the trap, because, as F1 indicates, Caliban speaks '*within*' before his entrance. But which one he uses is a crucial question. One is associated with authority, whereas the other is associated with the underworld. Interestingly, Caliban is entitled to use both entryways. The question, then, is which interpretation of Caliban—i.e. the rightful owner of the island or a bastard by the devil—is emphasized by his entrance. The use of the central doorway would suggest the validity of his claim to the island and, therefore, the ambiguity of Prospero's authority. At the end everyone exits through the same central opening into Prospero's 'cell'. The entryways that Prospero and Caliban use for their first appearances contribute to the establishment of their status and character and hence, by extension, to our interpretation of the play as a whole.

Harmonious General Exits. At the ends of the romantic comedies and some other plays, the central opening is fit for the joint departure of the two groups of characters who have achieved a harmonious relationship. Our final suggestion is that, whether regal or not, the general exits at the ends of these plays are made through the central opening. The last scene of *Henry V* begins with a split entrance of English and French characters. In this scene, Henry's conquest of France and the peace between England and France are established through the marriage contract between Henry and Katherine. It is likely that the central opening is used for the final general exit as a signal of the achieved harmony.

Other plays forsake the flanking doors for the central opening for similar symbolic reasons. We have already mentioned the likelihood that the central opening is used for the general exit in the finale of *The Tempest*. This is mainly because the central opening would most fittingly represent the entrance to Prospero's cell, but also because the centre would fit an exit signifying reunion and reconciliation. Caliban is dismissed into Prospero's cell some twenty lines earlier, while Prospero remains for another twenty lines to speak the Epilogue, which separates each of them from the general harmonization.

It seems also likely that in the finale of *The Merchant of Venice*, when Portia suggests going into her house to other characters, she leads them to the central opening. As in the finales of *The Two Gentlemen of Verona* and *The Merry Wives of Windsor*, even where the general exit is made as a return journey, it seems likely that the central opening is used for the exit. These are harmonious, unified closures. By contrast, at the end of *Love's Labour's Lost*, where 'Jacke hath not Gill' (5.2.862), the king and three lords of Navarre and the queen and three ladies of France would probably exit by opposing doors, each group followed by either the characters who have sung the song of spring or those who have sung the song of winter.[36] We believe that, except for the cases where the central opening cannot be used,[37] at the ends of comedies characters usually exited through the harmonious central space.

We have suggested several likely tactics here: (1) that the central opening would have represented the entrance to a recessed place and the gates of a fortress; (2) that the action of hiding behind the hangings could have been regarded as an exit; (3) that the central opening would have been used for masques and shows; (4) that the central opening might have been used by special figures, such as supernatural beings and Choruses; (5) that the centre would have been most appropriate for formal and ceremonial processions; and (6) that the central opening would have served a symbolic function. We must admit that there are very few instances where we can claim with total confidence that the central opening was used for an entrance or exit. In the above-mentioned instances, it is not absolutely necessary for any enterer or exiter to use the central opening. If we took a minimalist attitude, we should have to abandon these speculations as unproven. However, since the central opening was available as a third entryway, it seems reasonable to speculate that, except when the company was on its travels and had to perform in a space with limited resources, the central opening would have served as the special and authoritative entry and exit point.

The Timing and Style of Entrances and Exits

a. Timing

A systematic check of the lines allocated in the original texts for characters to make their exits and entrances gives us a clear idea of the timing that they were expected to require. In many cases several interpretations of the timing are possible, sometimes with intriguing implications for the overriding intention. But even the most unclear cases show how important were the timing and the text's location of its stage directions, given the large size of the amphitheatre stages.

Consider, for instance, this passage from *Hamlet* Q2.

> *Ham.* O good *Horatio,* Ile take the Ghosts word for a
>   thousand pound. Did'st perceive?
> *Hora.* Very well my Lord.
> *Ham.* Upon the talke of the poysning.
> *Hor.* I did very well note him.
> *Ham.* Ah ha, come some musique, come the Recorders,
>   For if the King like not the Comedie,
>   Why then belike he likes it not perdy.
>   Come, some musique.
>   *Enter Rosencraus and Guyldensterne.*
> *Guyl.* Good my Lord, voutsafe me a word with you.
>
>   (3.2.274–84)

The Q2 text, which is thought to be based upon Shakespeare's foul papers, places the entry stage direction for Rosencrantz and Guildenstern just before their first speech. On the other hand, the F1 text, which is thought to have been printed from a transcript of the playbook reflecting the revision of the Q2 version by Shakespeare himself, places the same entry stage direction four lines earlier. The two texts provide substantially the same dialogue. It seems most reasonable to think that since Shakespeare did not change the dialogue in this passage when he revised the original version, his intention was, in both versions, to make Rosencrantz and Guildenstern enter at the point indicated by the F1 stage direction so that the students might join Hamlet at the point indicated by the Q2 stage direction. But it is also possible to treat each stage direction in its own right, because Q2 and F1 offer different versions of the staging.

Suppose that in the Q2 version Rosencrantz and Guildenstern enter through the flanking 'entrance door' at the moment that the entry stage direction indicates. In this case, the dialogue indicates that Hamlet is expressing the great satisfaction he has got from the success of *The Mousetrap* by calling for music and parodying lines from *The Spanish Tragedy*. These lines would serve quite well as the conclusion to the dialogue between Hamlet and Horatio, and therefore of the *Mousetrap* episode. This is an acceptable interpretation, though it does not entirely explain why Hamlet utters the interjection 'Ah ha'. On the other hand, in the F1 version, Hamlet must deliberately ignore the arrival of Rosencrantz and Guildenstern. This version also links Horatio's 'note' with a pun by Hamlet, to the effect that the students are the 'recorders' or spies of his actions. He amplifies this challenging attitude towards them by parodying the lines from *The Spanish Tragedy* and inventing the couplet about the King's dislike of the play. Although Hamlet's speech is substantially the same in both versions, the alteration of the timing of the arrival of Rosencrantz and Guildenstern changes his meaning quite markedly.

For another example take Gloucester's blind exit in the Q1 version of *King Lear*.

> *Glost.* O my follies, then *Edgar* was abus'd,
> Kinde Gods forgive me that, and prosper him.
> *Reg.* Goe thrust him out at gates, and let him smell his
> way to Dover, how ist my Lord? how looke you?

> *Corn.* I have receiv'd a hurt, follow me Ladie,
> Turne out that eyles villaine, throw this slave upon
> The dungell *Regan*, I bleed apace, untimely
> Comes this hurt, give me your arme.   *Exit.*
> *Servant.* Ile never care what wickednes I doe,
> If this man come to good.
> *2 Servant.* If she live long, & in the end meet the old
> course of death, women will all turne monsters.
> *1 Ser.* Lets follow the old Earle, and get the bedlom
> To lead him where he would, his rogish madnes
> Allows it selfe to any thing.
> *2 Ser.* Goe thou, ile fetch some flaxe and whites of egges
> to apply to his bleeding face, now heaven helpe him.
>   *Exit.*
>   (14.89–105)

The Q1 text, which is thought to be based on Shakespeare's foul papers or early draft of the play, gives no stage direction for Gloucester's exit. It is therefore reasonable to suppose that one of the on-stage servants had the task of mutely unbinding Gloucester and leading him away just after Regan's command, which is where the F1 text places their exit. The F1 dialogue around the stage direction is substantially the same as the Q1 version, so this may be no more than a playhouse augmentation. However, the dialogue of the remaining servants is given only in the Q1 version. F1's placing of Gloucester's exit may be connected with its omission of the dialogue. For practical reasons, the slowness of Gloucester's exit might well have been avoided towards the end of the scene in the F1 version, especially if an act-break was inserted into the later version of the play after the departure of Cornwall, Regan, and others.[1] Assuming that Q1 and F1 are different versions, it seems equally likely that, in the Q1 version, when Cornwall repeats Regan's command two lines later, the servant is still untying Gloucester. An alternative possibility is that the servants are so shocked and intimidated by what they have seen that none of them can even begin to unbind Gloucester until Cornwall gives the same order a second time.[2] Although in the Q1 version we cannot be sure at which moment the servant and Gloucester should begin to depart, the servant's delay in obeying Regan's command would emphasize the inhumanity of Regan and Cornwall.

In the Q1 version Gloucester's exit might have taken longer than in the F1 version, for the First Servant's 'Lets follow the old Earle' may imply that Gloucester has not yet completely gone from the stage at that moment. It may be that the Q1 version was designed to give Cornwall's servants three kinds of critical attitude towards their master and mistress: opposition to Cornwall's attempt to put out the other eye of Gloucester, delay in obeying Regan's command, and comment on the moral degeneracy of Cornwall and Regan. These critical attitudes, based on the servants' sympathy for Gloucester, emphasize the monstrosity of Regan and Cornwall and also provide some relief within the scene. Whether Gloucester and the servant begin to depart just after Regan's command or, alternatively, do not begin to move until after Cornwall's command is not a trivial question. The effect of the one form of their exiting is quite different from the other form. Since Regan and Cornwall misuse and maim Gloucester as a substitute for Lear, the agony which Gloucester suffers is a part of Lear's tragedy. The F1 version makes this portion of the play much darker by cutting the servants' remarks about the inhumanity of their master and mistress and their good wishes for Gloucester.[3] This instance, like the one from *Hamlet* (3.2.274–84), shows how the timing of entrances and exits can influence the larger theatrical significance of the entrances and exits themselves and the meanings of the speeches around them.

b. Style and Form

A Midsummer Night's Dream F1 contains some intriguing examples of what might be called duplicated stage directions. It is generally agreed that the F1 text was printed from an exemplar of Q2 annotated from a playhouse manuscript and that Q2 is a reprint edition of Q1, behind which lies Shakespeare's foul papers. One oddity is in 3.1, where F1 adds '*Enter Pucke*' (3.1.49), but also retains Q2's '*Enter Robin*' (3.1.70). In 4.1, F1 mentions Oberon's name in the following two stage directions: '*Enter Queene of Fairies, and Clowne, and Fairies, and the King behinde them*' (4.1.0); '*Enter Robin goodfellow and Oberon*' (4.1.44). In this case, F1 retains Q2's earlier entry for Oberon, but also gives him a later entry. It is very likely that the F1 retentions of Q2's later entry for Robin and earlier entry for Oberon are passive errors in the printing process on the part of either the collator or compositor.[4] Robin's early entrance in 3.1 seems to reflect stage practice.[5] Although the audience is informed earlier in the play about the invisibility of the fairies, Robin would not approach the mechanicals immediately after his entrance but would watch them from near the *frons* or behind a stage post until he moves forward to take part in their rehearsal. If this is the case, on his entry in 4.1, Oberon may make a similar movement, i.e. enter at the opening of the scene, and observe the behaviour of Titania and Bottom from a distance on stage until they sleep and Robin arrives. In short, although the F1 retentions may be errors, in each case the two entries may work differently, the first indicating the arrival and the second indicating the action of coming forward.

In the opening scene of *Romeo and Juliet*, when Gregory says, 'Say better, here comes one of my maisters kinsmen' (1.1.55–6), he must be referring to Tybalt's arrival. However, in Q2 and F1, only Benvolio's entrance is marked just before this speech, and Tybalt's entrance is not marked until six lines after it. Here Shakespeare might have forgotten either that Gregory is a Capulet, or that Benvolio is a Montague.[6] Suppose that Tybalt enters at almost the same time as Benvolio does: he would probably enter from one flanking door as Benvolio enters from the other, using the Capulet side while Benvolio uses the Montague point of entry, or he would enter after Benvolio from the same door, keeping his distance; he would wait to come forward until the serving-men begin to fight and Benvolio draws his sword to part them. The difference between Benvolio's and Tybalt's movements would be nothing less than the contrast between their attitudes towards the fighting. It seems possible to conclude that the entry stage direction for Tybalt is used to indicate the moment when he, already on stage, should advance to join the action.

As suggested in the previous chapter, in *King Lear*, 3.4, the central opening may well represent the 'hovel' of Poor Tom, into which the Fool goes, and out of which he almost immediately emerges. When the Fool re-enters at line 36, according to the F1 text, Edgar enters with him ('*Enter Edgar, and Foole*'), although Kent subsequently bids Edgar to 'Come forth' at line 43. F1 gives Edgar one line to be spoken immediately after his entrance: 'Fathom, and halfe, Fathom and halfe; poore *Tom*' (3.4.37). In Q1, on the other hand, the entry stage direction for Edgar and the Fool at line 36 is omitted, and Edgar does not speak until he is told to 'come forth'. It may be that, at least in the F1 version,

Edgar was revealed when the Fool reappeared, but that he did not come out of the discovery space until after line 43. Amongst other examples, the opening stage direction of *Julius Caesar*, 3.3, '*Enter Cinna the Poet, and after him the Plebeians*' is very similar to the opening stage direction of *A Midsummer Night's Dream*, 4.1. Did the plebeians remain near their entry door until they began to speak to Cinna, or did they follow at his heels while he spoke his four-line 'soliloquy', unaware of them? It is also possible to think that the plebeians were intended to enter at line 4.[7] These different forms of entrance would procure entirely different effects.

We have already suggested the possibility that the F1 stage direction, '*Enter Hamlet and Horatio a farre off*' (*Hamlet*, 5.1.55), indicates that Hamlet and Horatio make what might be called a broken entrance. This stage direction is marked nine lines before Hamlet's first speech. In *All's Well That Ends Well* F1 there is another example of an entry stage direction (1.3.123) marked nine lines before the enterer's first speech. In this instance, Helen presumably makes a very slow or broken entrance.[8] Either manner of entrance seems fit to show her suffering from the pain of unrequited love. *Romeo and Juliet* Q2 has Romeo enter eight lines before he first speaks in 2.2; in *Measure for Measure*, 2.3, Juliet enters (2.3.9) eight lines earlier than she is addressed. Their very slow or broken entrances would have expressed their states of mind.

c. Entry-Point

Different entry-points give different meanings to an entrance or exit. In *The Tempest*, 1.2, as discussed in the previous chapter, the choice of entryway Prospero and Caliban use for their first appearances—a flanking door, the central opening, or the trap?—would have made a positive contribution to the establishment of their status and character. In 3.3 Prospero makes a very special entrance. The stage direction merely says, '*Solemne and strange Musicke: and Prospero on the top (invisible:)* . . .' (*The Tempest*, 3.3.17). J. C. Adams concluded that portions of the third-level façade in his reconstruction of the Globe opened to form a music gallery, and that Prospero appeared in front of the music curtains.[9] Stephen Orgel asserts that 'top' was 'a technical term for the level above the upper stage gallery, within which the musicians sat'.[10] An early Shakespearian play has another example which involves an entry on the 'top': *'Enter Pucell on the top, thrusting out a Torch burning'* (*1 Henry VI*, 3.3.8). Michael Hattaway suggests the possibility that the Pucell appeared in the hut above the 'heavens'.[11] Such a high place might have been an appropriate entry-point for characters with supernatural power when their powers were being used: for the Pucell to give a signal to the characters below, and for Prospero to oversee the action on the stage beneath him. But whether the 'top' was the balcony or elsewhere is uncertain. We are sceptical about a special place for the 'top'. Whether *The Tempest* was written specifically for the Blackfriars or not, the musicians were occupying the balcony in the Globe when *The Tempest* was performed there. We think that Prospero appeared on the balcony among or in front of the musicians. He does not speak until about twenty lines after his entrance. Assuming that he appears on the balcony, the music provided there would draw the audience's attention to his presence. If the musicians were behind the curtains and needed signals for music and sound, as Adams convincingly argues, Prospero could give them such signals there.[12] It may be significant that the stage direction does not include the word *'enter'*. Assuming the balcony was furnished with curtains, behind which the musicians played, Prospero could have been discovered.

  Our goal here is not to choose the one and only 'authentic' form of each particular entrance or exit. The object is to provide means by which to recover possible effects and meanings in the entrances and exits that the original audience of Shakespeare would have appreciated. The Globe playhouse, now reconstructed in Southwark, will serve as a laboratory, in which some of the theories set out here will be tested. This will show how the chosen timing, manner, and entry-point of a particular entrance or exit can influence our perception of it.

The Early Staging of Hamlet

a. *Hamlet* as an Act

All theatre is about seeming and pretence. Shakespeare and some of his peers called it counterfeiting, passing false coin on the pretence that it is genuine. *Hamlet* is largely about that concept of acting as deception, its narrative the pretend performance of an 'act' of revenge, in which a play-actor enacts actions that a man might *play*, unseriously. Through the first half of the play Hamlet himself is constantly exercised to question the seeming and deception surrounding him at Elsinore. In the original staging the element of metatheatre in all that pretence was underlined for the audience from the opening words. The curt exchange between the sentries in the first six lines spoken tells us that it is very late at night ('Tis now struck twelve'), and that 'Tis bitter cold'. The night when the play opens is too dark for the sentry and his relief to identify each other except by their voices. The first audiences who heard and saw this were at the Globe on the Bankside in London in broad daylight, at 2 p.m. probably on a hot summer's afternoon. They were being asked to imagine that it was the opposite.

What the scene actually is and what it seems to be, what the audience is asked to believe for the moment that it is supposed to be, were features of the original staging much more obviously at odds for the first audiences than they are now to audiences who have cinematic aids to satisfy their imaginations. When Hamlet in the second scene picks up his mother's word about his mood seeming dark and throws it back at her ('Nay madam, it *is*, I know not "seems"'), he calls attention to the difference between clothing and the reality it covers. He is acting out the truth of his feelings in his dress whatever the contrasting colours of the wedding's celebrants may seem to signify. Reminders of such role-playing and game-playing on the stage were a constant element in the original performance of *Hamlet*.

The reconstruction of the original staging which follows is of course conjectural. The best that can be said for it is that it follows the best-guess principle that led to the finished design of the new Globe in Southwark, and that in making its guesses it has taken into account all of the most recent and intensive debates about the nature of Tudor staging practices. Where tangible evidence exists, it is cited. Where equivalent features exist that might indicate significant alternative ways of doing the staging at that point, they are acknowledged. It should be added that it is a guess at an optimal performance, without any of the cuts and shortening that most early performances must have undergone.

One major feature of the staging that is necessarily conjectural is the choice of the flanking stage doors, left and right, for routine entrances. This is part of a complex argument, still in progress, about what were the players' standard practices in the tiring house when they had to choose which flanking door to enter and exit by. *Hamlet* is by no means the only play where chaos would have followed if one actor had gone to the wrong door for his exit and bumped into the actor entering to start the next scene. The Elizabethan players must have had rules of thumb to cope with such potential clashes. Different theories have been broached to satisfy this. Bernard Beckerman proposed that an actor would routinely exit by the opposite door to the one he had come in by, the 'O' rule.[1] The opposite rule is the 'S' rule, where an actor exits by the same door that he had entered by. Neither rule, unfortunately, works with perfect consistency in any play. An alternative is a location rule, which we might call the 'L' rule, where one door represents the outside world and the other door the inner, so that a character entering from indoors and then going out on a journey would always come in by the 'inner' door and go out by the 'outer'.[2] This means of differentiating the two doors might work with *Macbeth*, and a few other plays. But again, it does not work with sufficient consistency to be acknowledged as the players' invariable rule of thumb for choosing which door to enter or exit by.

Given the limited time for rehearsal, some standard rule of thumb must have been used to denote which door a player would go to. In

scenes where one entering character was required to meet one departing, for instance, both players must have known which door to use.
Finding what rules of this kind the players worked to is one of the
major challenges to future research on early staging practices.[3] However identifying what became the Tudor rule of thumb, O, S, L, or any
other, for working out entrances and exits is only one of many problems relating to the players entering and leaving the stage: the largest
of all is the possible use of the central opening in the *frons*. It was an
exceptionally broad opening, and being central it had a symbolic role
signifying harmony which should not be ignored. Quite apart from the
early tradition of using the hangings that fronted the booth on mar-
ket-place stages for all entries and exits, as in Dutch paintings of
staging at country fairs,[4] there is evidence to suggest that, even after
the two flanking doors became available for standard entries, some
clowns still used to enter by first sticking their heads out through the
hangings that fronted the central opening.[5] Conceivably this tradition
developed as a deliberate opposite, a carnivalesque parody, of the
central opening's normal use for ceremonial entrances by authority
figures.

We would expect royal entrances to be made through the wide
central opening, hirelings holding the curtains back for the 'discovery'
of the grandeur entering. The many plays which used two opposing
parties, Yorkists against Lancastrians, Montagues against Capulets,
Oberons against Titanias, might normally have used the two flanking
doors to identify each other by where they entered and exited. That
would have freed the central opening for the authority figures like the
Duke of Verona and Theseus. It would also suit Oberon with Titania,
once they had reunited, to signal their new unity by making their final
collective exits, hand-in-hand and reharmonized, through the central
opening. The same harmony could be shown with a hand-in-hand
central exit by the four newly united or reunited pairs of lovers in *A
Midsummer Night's Dream*. Romantic comedies called for a public
show of marital harmony at the conclusion. By contrast, the departures
in *Love's Labour's Lost*, 'You that way, we this way', signal the absence of
marital harmony by separate exits through the flanking doors.[6]

Such a reading of the possible uses of the three openings in the *frons*
is inferential, and by its nature inconclusive. None the less, it seems the
best way to reconcile the demands of the text with what we know about

the design of the stage and its *frons*. Other problems about entrances and exits are more down-to-earth. There is, for instance, little to say whether the flanking doors were normally shut, or were curtained, or were open spaces in the *frons*. Assuming that there were doors, were they normally closed or open? Did the blue-coated stage-hands[7] stand by to open them on demand, as they did when they 'discovered' spectacles by pulling back the stage hangings? Or did the actors handle the doors themselves? The cumulative evidence suggests that the flanking doorways did have doors hung on them, and the logic of keeping what was going on backstage from the eyes of the groundlings argues that they would normally have been kept closed. While ceremonial entrances by royalty through the central opening would have called for hands to hold the curtains back, there would be nothing but trouble and crowding if the flanking doors were constantly attended by the stage hands. Solo scenes with soliloquies, even when spoken at the 'front' edge of the stage, would seem awkward if attendants were present by the doors. Court scenes would routinely have had servants standing by the *frons* ready for use as messengers or to run errands, and to carry off the royal dais when the king left. For intimate scenes such as those between Romeo and Juliet hirelings on stage would have been an intrusion. Solo players must have opened their own doors.

In what follows we assume that such practices were standard, and we indicate whether any different form of entry from the solo door-opening system is likely for any scene. We have made a rather arbitrary choice, for the two flanking doors, marking them 'L' and 'R', which might be either stage left and right or audience left and right. It is the opposition of the two openings, and their distance from each other, that counts. If the principle of the 'L' rule has any value at all, we might claim that the door we designate L usually leads inwards, while the door R leads outwards.

The other and less than arbitrary marker is the indication of 'front' and 'back'. Even with the lords' rooms and the highest-paying customers sitting in the *frons*, thinking of a truly round theatre and stage as having a front and a back is inadequate. To avoid confusion, we reluctantly adopt here the modern terminology, and call the stage edge where there was most room for the groundlings to stand the 'front'.

The three texts of *Hamlet* reflect different staging intentions. They start with the second quarto (Q2), printed from what was very likely Shakespeare's initial manuscript as it was originally delivered to the players. This quarto shows little sign of any work done to prepare the play for staging. Differing in significant ways is the First Folio text (F1), printed in 1623 from a playhouse manuscript which appears to have been marked up and altered over the years for staging in ways that change the text in several places from the Q2 version. Thirdly there is the first quarto (Q1), which records a not very grammatical version of the text, but which has a number of stage directions noting distinctive features of the 1603 or earlier staging. There are signs that the F text prints alterations relating to staging that were added to its manuscript from performances dating well after the Q1 staging, possibly at any time in the decade up to 1623. For quotations from the text here, we have used the First Folio as the nearest to the text as normally staged, adding stage directions from Q1 and Q2 whenever they appear to add anything significant to the F text.

The account is divided into sections by the conventional but post-Shakespeare sequence of Acts. In print, the play's division into acts was first made in the quarto of 1676, and has the authority only of proscenium-arch staging. The first editors of the copy for F made a rudimentary attempt at finding act and scene divisions, but gave up at 2.2. We use the conventional act and scene-numbering here, following Oxford's divisions, for simplicity of reference, since every editor since Rowe in 1709 has broken the text into acts and scenes. The original performances flowed continuously, without any breaks either in the form of a central interval or as pauses between the acts.

b. Act 1

We imagine the play beginning, after the trumpets have sounded three times to command silence from the audience,[8] with Barnardo entering L and Francisco R. There are no attendants at the doors. Each entrant is dressed as a soldier, and carries a halberd, a long-handled spear or pike with a large cutting blade at the top. Francisco stands still by the *frons*, holding his halberd at the ready. He starts when Barnardo, creeping carefully along the *frons* towards him holding the point of his halberd forward, gives the challenge. His response is prompt, and corrective. He is the one on guard who should be issuing the challenge, not his relief. He only relaxes when Barnardo gives the password, 'Long live the King', and says reprovingly that he is only just on his hour. They stay by the *frons* for the brief exchange which tells us the time of night and the weather, Francisco saying there have been no alarms in his watch. He says farewell and makes for the door L by which Barnardo had entered. As he does so, Horatio and Marcellus come out of it, and Francisco gives them the challenge.

Horatio is dressed as a gentleman, in a velvet doublet and cloak, with a feathered hat. He has a gentleman's rapier at his side. Marcellus is a soldier dressed better than the sentries and carrying a 'partisan', a slimmer version of the halberd and the mark of a junior officer. Once Francisco has gone out by the door L, the two soldiers move to the front of the stage with Horatio to discuss what they have come for, hunching down together and facing each other as Barnardo begins to tell Horatio about the ghost. Marcellus, the one with his back to the stage's front edge, is the first to see the ghost climb up from the trapdoor in centre stage. They all spring erect, facing it. Horatio is pushed forward to address it, but it moves away, through the door R by which Francisco the sentinel on duty first entered.

The ghost is in armour, helmeted, with 'his Beaver up', as Horatio later describes it to Hamlet, and carries the baton or 'Truncheon' of a field general in charge of an army. It returns to them through the same door while they are talking, and makes a gesture described in the Q2 stage direction as '*It spreads his armes*', a gesture of defeat or appeal, in place of speaking. As they try to bar its way with their pikes, pretending blindness in the ostensible dark and milling around the stage posts to add to the confusion, it goes back down the trap. They draw together to talk about it, and once Horatio has proposed a course of action, which is to tell young Hamlet about the ghost—checking with the soldiers, the King's guards, that it fits their soldierly duty to do so—they all exit by the door L.

The second scene is a total contrast to the frightened scurrying in the dark of the first scene. A major crowd scene, laden with a public show of ceremony, it starts with a trumpet flourish. Formal entries and exits by royalty were always signalled in this way. A 'flourish' was an announcement that the monarch was about to enter.[9] There is no stage direction for one here, either in F1 or Q2, but the '*flourish*' they provide for Claudius and Gertrude's exit is needed for the entry too. While the trumpet sounds, two stage-hands draw the curtains back from the central opening. Other hands enter through the central opening carrying the dais and its two painted and canopied wooden chairs, the royal thrones. The dais is placed a little back from centre stage, over the trapdoor and facing the yard.[10] King Claudius and Queen Gertrude enter through the same opening, followed by the court, and sit on the two chairs of state. Claudius is never named in any speech in the play. The only time his name appears in any of the texts is in this opening stage direction in Q2. The name Claudius, a change from the source's Fengon, was probably introduced as a characteristically oblique reference to the classical precedents for Hamlet's conduct, as in the verses about the death of King Priam. Claudius was uncle to Nero, whom Hamlet mentions as his role model when he goes to visit his mother. In Q2's stage direction his name is used rather than his title, although his ceremonial dress as king would have been the strongest feature of his appearance on stage at the Globe. Gertrude, as Claudius announces, is 'Th'Imperiall Joyntresse of this warlike State', an equal ranking which puts her alongside the king, while also raising a hint of doubt about what question of succession the speedy marriage might have shut off.

The king and queen wear crowns, Polonius wears his robe and chain of office with its gold seal on his breast, and carries the staff of a chamberlain. All the courtiers except for Hamlet are dressed colourfully, since they come from the royal wedding. The male courtiers stand facing the thrones hat in hand. The hangings are drawn shut after the procession, and all but the royal pair group themselves round the periphery of the stage, facing the dais, waiting for the king to speak. The stage-hands stand as attendants along the *frons* behind the thrones.

Claudius has not been named, so an attentive hearer might expect him to be the young Hamlet whom Horatio has just named and proposed to inform about the ghost. That expectation would be knocked away when the king speaks his first line about '*Hamlet* our deere *Brothers* death'. The new king is not the son of the dead king. His speech first announces the completion of the customary period of mourning and its replacement by the wedding celebrations. The next item on the agenda is the threat from young Fortinbras, who like young Hamlet is his king's nephew, a threat which Claudius deals with by sending ambassadors to inform the Norwegian king of the danger that Fortinbras's plan to invade poses to Denmark. From his throne, Claudius makes light of the danger with a slightly ponderous joke. When he says that the plotting Fortinbras is taking the chance of Denmark being in disarray,

> thinking by our late deere Brothers death,
> Our State to be disjoynt, and out of Frame,

he pats the arm of his own 'state', the chair of state that he is sitting on, which is self-evidently not coming apart at the joints. He confirms how completely he is in control by announcing his counter-plot to foil Fortinbras. Voltemand and Cornelius enter L when summoned by one of the attendants standing by the *frons*, and kneel to Claudius to receive their commissions for journeying to Norway. It is likely that the player of Voltemand also played Marcellus. This doubling required him to be allowed about twenty-five lines to change his appearance, the amount allowed for Jessica's disguise in *The Merchant of Venice* at 2.6.1–25, rather more than for Ariel's main costume changes in *The Tempest*, at 1.2.307–20 and 4.1.143–64. A pause for the change of costume explains why the ambassadors did not enter with the other courtiers.

As they exit by the other door Claudius turns to deal with Laertes, and finally Hamlet, who has stood to one side during all this court business. When summoned, Laertes comes to the chair of state and kneels, a markedly different show of bodily respect from Hamlet's silent discourtesy.

The early texts disagree about the order of entry for this scene, and about Hamlet's position. The second quarto, from the author's manu-script, names him last, as if he was supposed to enter out of his ranking place in the royal procession. The Folio text accords him his proper ranking in the sequence, immediately after Gertrude and before Polo-nius. The Q2 version cannot be seen as a definite indication of the author's plan, since the names may simply follow the sequence in which the characters speak during the scene. It would, though, be a pointed act if Hamlet ignored his proper place in the procession. He would be out of step, dressed in black mourning for his father while everyone else has changed into their most handsome clothes for the wedding.

Whichever version was right, he stands apart from the assembly through the early part of the scene, beside the crowd in the yard, refusing to look directly at the occupants of the two thrones. When Claudius finally turns in his speech to address Hamlet he tacitly acknowledges his out-of-place stance by summoning him only after he has dealt with the lesser figure of Laertes. He then reverses that demotion by proclaiming that despite it, in the elective kingdom of Denmark,[11] young Hamlet is the successor he has chosen, and is to be treated as such:

> For let the world take note,
> You are the most immediate to our Throne,
> And with no lesse Nobility of Love,
> Then that which deerest Father beares his Sonne,
> Do I impart towards you.

Claudius makes a wide gesture to the surround of courtiers as he orders the world to take note of his weighty proclamation.

During this public address to him Hamlet's attitude is far less gracious than Claudius's and far less decorous than Laertes's. It reflects his body language up to now, standing aloof, refusing to face the throne as all the other courtiers are doing, possibly facing sideways, out of place behind the other courtiers. Standing there, his asides would thus be directed towards the audience in the yard rather than to where the other players are facing. It was distinctly improper behaviour for a courtier, and certainly for a figure just named as heir to the throne. It gives point to the fact that this 'young Hamlet' is not the man sitting on the throne of Denmark, any more than 'young Fortinbras', a man who occupies an evidently equivalent position to young Hamlet, sits on the Norwegian throne.

The court leaves ceremoniously, again with the exception of Hamlet, processing back through the central opening with another flourish of trumpets and attendant stage hands, who close the hangings as they follow the last pair of courtiers out. The stage is now empty except for Hamlet, who starts his soliloquy from the stage front, explaining the reason for his dissonant behaviour to the audience around him. Where Claudius spoke to the assembled court around his throne, Hamlet addresses the real audience, moving across the edges of the stage and addressing the groundlings around him directly. His gesture on saying 'to this' (1.2.139), in comparing his father to his uncle, is a fling of a disdainful arm back towards the hangings where Claudius exited.

On Horatio and his companions' entry through door R a neat little status game follows. Horatio brings the soldiers to Hamlet, offering him a formal greeting. Hamlet responds, then does a double take, recognizing not just another courtier but his friend. He insists on converting Horatio's bow of lower status as a 'servant' into the embrace of equal friends. The officer Marcellus he greets more distantly, as more of a 'servant', by naming him. The soldier Barnardo he even more remotely acknowledges by giving him merely the time of day (the afternoon).[12] Horatio does not identify him to Hamlet as Barnardo for another thirty lines. This marking of three separate social levels Hamlet alters as they leave him to exit by their entry door R when he dismisses their servant-like gestures of 'duty', which echo the reason they agreed amongst themselves for telling their story only to Hamlet, not the king. Hamlet unknowingly comments on that by insisting their relationship is the 'love' of equals, not the duty of royal servants. He then makes his own exit by door L.

As he leaves, Laertes and his sister enter in mid-conversation with each other through door R. They wear the courtly dress of the previous scene as young nobles. Laertes is dressed in riding boots for travel with a rapier at his side, and their talk is intimate, between family members. Polonius, now without his chamberlain's insignia, but still wearing the large bonnet of his quasi-judicial role at court, enters by the same door. They all stand, for intimacy, in centre-stage, between the stage posts. Polonius is as warm and familiar to his children as they are to each other, though both bow their heads and bend a knee slightly on seeing him, in acknowledgement of his authority as their father. In every way, although similarly located in centre-stage, this scene contrasts with the two that went before. Those scenes used the whole stage, either through violent movement or through the size of the cluster of characters. This is intimate conversation, an exchange between family members whose distinct identities are immediately clear, and whose relations are touched with delicate comedy. Ophelia is starting to

follow after her brother on his outward journey when Polonius calls
her back. After her quiet firmness in turning Laertes's pomposities
back on himself, Ophelia's obedience to her father ('I shall obey, my
Lord', 1.3.136) emphasizes the sense of normal relationships based on
duty which Hamlet has already called in question in his insistence to
Horatio's group that he sees love not duty as what matters. When
Polonius says 'Come your wayes' and they both start to exit by the door
(L), opposite to the one Laertes went out by, Ophelia's obedience is
signalled by a formal curtsey.

Scene 4 returns to the mood of the opening, a bitter cold night on
the battlements. We are reminded of the ostensible chill and the late
hour, and see Hamlet now joined with those he identifies as his
friends. Again, they stand well forward of the *frons*, in front of the
stage posts. The noise of trumpets and drums from off-stage behind
the *frons* emphasises their remoteness from the court and its sociable
drinking. The ghost can thus enter from the centre-stage trap behind
them, as before. He leads Hamlet off stage by the door R, followed by
Horatio and Marcellus, who have to wait a moment on stage after they
have gone when Hamlet draws his sword to keep his 'friends' back.
The ghost then re-enters by the other door still followed by Hamlet,
sword in hand. In mid-stage Hamlet stops, saying 'Speak; Ile go no
further.' The sword, which he soon sheathes and forgets once he hears
what the ghost has to say, makes an ironic comment on the order to kill
Claudius.

The ghost goes down the trap when he says he scents the morning
air, and Hamlet stands near the hole in centre stage to voice his
reactions. First he uses both hands to make a vivid visual gesture,
putting his hands to his head as he says

> Remember thee?
> I, thou poore Ghost, while memory holds a seate
> In this distracted Globe: Remember thee?

The gesture affirms the fourfold visual and verbal pun of clutching his
head, an orb driven to distraction. The round shape on his shoulders
signifies the world and the playhouse as well as his own head. It also
broaches as a visual pun the second of his own three comparisons of
himself with Hercules, the classical man of action who, in contrast to
the struggling Hamlet, succeeded in completing his twelve impossible

labours. Hamlet makes four references in all to Hercules. At the first, in the second scene of the play, he says he is as unlike Hercules as his uncle is to his father. His second is to the Nemean lion, another labour and source of the lion skin which Hercules wore. The third is this exclamation, and the fourth is Hamlet's parting jibe after the fight with Laertes/Hercules in Ophelia's grave, a mixture of bravado and mockery: 'Let *Hercules* himselfe doe what he may, | The Cat will Mew, and Dogge will have his day.'

In this reference, the head on Hamlet's shoulders is the burden of the globe, like the one held briefly by Hercules. If, as is now generally agreed, the Globe's motto and the insignia on its flag was an image of Hercules carrying the globe on his shoulders, this complex tripartite pun included a fourth element, a tightly local in-joke about the playhouse's emblem.[13] Like all the other metatheatrical jokes with which the play is packed, it bonds into the other recurrent motifs of the story.

Hamlet speaks this at the front of the stage, with a post between him and the door L from which Horatio and Marcellus call off-stage. They burst in still calling, using the cry commonly used to summon a hawk, which Hamlet responds to. They meet at front stage, and exchange wild and whirling words. Hamlet swears by St Patrick, traditionally the patron of mistakes and confusion, and guardian of the ghost's home, Purgatory. He draws his sword to make them swear secrecy on its cross-shaped hilt, and the '*Ghost cries under the Stage*' for them to swear as they start to do so. Hamlet moves them across the stage, and the ghost moves under the stage with them. The third time they move to centre stage, over the trap, and the fourth time near the *frons*, each time followed by the voice of the understage ghost. Hamlet tells them of his plan to disguise himself with an 'antic disposition', a stage clown's act. This not only puts his metatheatrical exhibition of play-acting into practice by explicitly acting a stage role but serves as an ironic version of what Philip Sidney objected to in his *Apology for Poetry*, published five years earlier. Sidney voiced a dislike of common plays which set clowns on stage to converse with kings. Hamlet will enact both ends of the social scale at once, and make himself a royal clown. But before he puts on such a peculiarly alienating role, we see he is no longer quite alone. At the end of the scene, when Hamlet says 'Nay, come let's goe together', Horatio the gentleman and Marcellus the king's officer go off quickly by the L door with him. This is the first time that Hamlet makes an exit in company with anyone other than the ghost.

c. Act 2

The second act begins with Polonius and Reynaldo entering L in conversation. After more of the comic by-play which marks all the Polonius scenes, Reynaldo exits R as Ophelia enters L in agitation. Her description of Hamlet in his antic (clown's) disposition, more truly identifiable as lunacy to judge from her description of him as hatless, with open doublet and foul and unlaced hose, describes the 'show' that the antic Hamlet has been putting on for the innocent. Ophelia is still the passively dutiful daughter, in marked contrast to Juliet and Desdemona and all of Shakespeare's comic heroines from Hermia to Rosalind, all of whom disobey their fathers for love. If it were not Polonius who reached the conclusion that Hamlet must have been driven mad by frustrated love, we might believe it too. Father and daughter go off together by the R door to tell the king. Polonius is fired with his urgent duty to do what Marcellus and Horatio have proved so oddly reluctant over.

The second scene of the second act shows us where Claudius is, in another court scene, to judge by Q2's '*Florish*' of trumpets for the formal entry through the central opening, and F's '*Cum aliis*', the usual parade of royal attendants. The dais with its chairs is brought on-stage for the royal pair to sit on. From there Claudius and Gertrude receive Hamlet's fellow-students from Wittenberg. First Rosencrantz and Guildenstern, kneeling before the dais, are welcomed, and then Polonius enters to announce the success of the mission to old Norway, and to tantalize his master with a trailer for his main feature. He first enters at L, the door the students entered by, as they leave R. He departs L and returns with the ambassadors. The Norwegian threat is dismissed, Fortinbras having submitted to his uncle the king, and Polonius can deliver his feature show. He does this standing in front of the royal dais and facing it, his back to the yard. He holds his rod of office and does not kneel, remaining on his feet because he is so much more senior than the students or the ambassadors, and is not asking for anything. The dais being near the centre of the stage allows him to strut across the front stage by the groundlings as he pontificates, his body language a joy to everyone.

This royal court scene does not end with the same sort of ceremony as the first one, nor the fuss of its opening. No trumpets sound, and there is no procession. Claudius leaves hastily, going behind the dais on seeing Hamlet enter hatless and unbraced as Ophelia had described him, another explicit mark of indecorum in the presence chamber, and '*reading on a Booke*'. In the 1570s Sir Thomas Smith reported of the English throne-room that 'in the chamber of presence where the cloath of estate is set, no man dare walke, yea though the prince be not there, no man dare tarrie there but bareheaded'.[14] For mad Hamlet to enter bareheaded so that he lacked a hat to doff was equally offensive.

Taking Gertrude's hand Claudius hurries her through the arras held open for them by the attendant stagehands, who vanish after them. Already Hamlet is beginning to disrupt royal ceremony. The thrones stand empty while Hamlet walks from the door L up the side of the stage past the nearer post, musing or pretending to muse (to read silently was uncommon). Polonius, now carrying his large bonnet in his hand, unlike hatless Hamlet, accosts him at the 'front' of the stage, forward of the posts.

After their exchange, Polonius moves back diagonally across the width of the stage towards the door R, where he meets Rosencrantz and Guildenstern as they enter. He gives them the few muttered statements of the obvious that he cannot resist before he exits and they cross the stage to Hamlet. He greets the two of them exactly as he had greeted Horatio, with the hand-clasp of 'friends'. They exchange their student wordplay and badinage, until the question of status accidentally intrudes. Hamlet says 'shall we to th'Court', meaning the lawcourt where their logic-chopping belongs, but they misunderstand, and both reply 'Wee'l wait upon you', a phrase that belongs at the royal court. This brings Hamlet up, and he says he will not put them with his other servants, as if they were waiters at court. He prefers 'the beaten way of friendship', and tests their honesty by asking them directly if they came as friends or because Claudius sent for them. Unlike Horatio, they fail the test. He starts play-acting, to confuse them, making his elaborate speech about 'this goodly frame the Earth', with its 'Canopy the Ayre', and 'this Majesticall Roofe, fretted with golden fire'. Each of these terms is accompanied by a gesture to the relevant features of the theatre, first round the whole auditorium, then to the stage cover, and then pointing to the gold painted frets picked out in the colouring of the stage heavens. His act prepares both naturally and metatheatrically for the arrival of the players.

This poorly-dressed group comes on stage by the door R, preluded by another trumpet-flourish, in involuntary parody of the two royal entries. Before they arrive Hamlet renews his own stage-playing by once again offering the hand of friendship to the two student-spies. He does so telling them that his true welcome for them must be matched by his false welcome to the players, '(which I tell you must shew fairly outward)'. This dialogue happens on the front edge of the stage, so they have ample time for their comments as Polonius enters R and approaches them to announce the players. They follow through the same door after some more of Hamlet's play-acting, this time fooling Polonius as a game for the two students. Hamlet is working a double level of deception. The different groupings, the uneasy pair of students, Hamlet, his blatant target Polonius, and what the Folio calls '*foure or five Players*', occupy the front stage forward of the posts. The player gives his 'rugged *Pyrrhus*' speech from centre stage, between and a little behind the stage posts, while Hamlet, Polonius and the two students occupy the stage edge looking back at him, the other players clustered to one side by a stage post.

The First Player's speech is much more stylized than anything that has gone before in the play, even Claudius's speech from the throne in 1.2. As an orator with a monologue he does not move about as much as the others do in their dialogue, though his arm gestures and body language are explicitly eloquent. Hamlet, having already play-acted two roles for the students and for Polonius, begins the process, speaking less extravagantly and with less movement than the Player, who takes the speech up in a more polished version of the same mode. Polonius praises his 'accent' or voice, not his 'action' or gesture in speaking. Echoing Marlowe's 'mighty line' in its insistent rhythm and its resonant nouns and adjectives, the Player's verse runs more slowly than the prose patter of the previous dialogue. The player has to use weighty pauses at the line-ends, especially after the short line 'did nothing', and for the echoic silence of the unspoken beats that follow the heavy line 'Now falles on *Priam*.'

Whether or not the audience is moved by the speech, Hamlet must be, since as he expected it provides an exact analogy to his duty as revenger, even in the long pause in the verse rhythm at 'did nothing'. When Polonius interrupts it, the audience ought to register the shallowness of his reaction in contrast with the insider's emotion. We must be on Hamlet's side by now, since we share the inside knowledge of all the characters that only he has on stage. Polonius's taste for jigs and bawdry, which Hamlet is later to deride when he reminds the players how they should act, does not belong with tragedy. The Player's tears as he goes on to speak of the grieving queen are more questionable, but they need comment since Hamlet has to acknowledge them as truer inward signs than the trappings and the suits of woe he had dismissed in his first appearance on stage. The Player is setting up a new level of the seeming and pretence which the whole play rides on. Whether the Player really weeps for Hecuba is a compressed clue in the game of counterfeiting which Hamlet is to broach in the soliloquy to follow: Hamlet distinguishes himself as real while the Player is a counterfeit, weeping for 'a Fixion, . . . a dreame of Passion'.[15] We have to remind ourselves that the distinction is itself a fiction.

From this fore-stage action, Polonius starts to lead the gentlemen off L, followed by the players, whom Hamlet now calls his 'Friends', as he had told his student-friends he must. This insistence on identifying friends is a recurrent feature of his early behaviour in the play. First he calls his fellow-student Horatio and the soldiers friends rather than men of humbler social status than himself, then the two additional students from Wittenberg, and now the players, the most obviously false pretenders to such a status. Except of course, that in metatheatrical thinking they must truly be his (Burbage's) fellows and friends.

When Hamlet holds the First Player back for the brief words which reveal how, for all the emotion, his mind is fixed on plotting his next moves, Polonius waits with the other players at the L door by the *frons*.[16] Hamlet speaks to the chief player at front-stage, well out of earshot of the group held standing in the distance waiting respectfully for Hamlet to finish. The soliloquy that he breaks into when they finally leave is a self-indulgence, a secret yet loud rant to the audience, the world outside Elsinore, at his being able, unlike Pyrrhus, not to do nothing but to '*say* nothing'. The action is already set up. He has moved to supply the players with his lines which will get Claudius to

admit his crime. It is the passion that he cannot express. To Elizabethans in an honest man the outward action, the external voice and
gesture, must reflect the inward passion. Not to do so is to adopt the
false poses of illusion and counterfeiting. Hamlet's complaint is that
he is forced into a position where he cannot be honest and speak his
mind. He is being made to behave like those seemers that he hates in
Elsinore. He leaves the stage, alone again, by the opposite door to the
others.

d. Act 3

The next scene, the beginning of Act 3, is not a ceremonial royal entry,
although the king and queen do enter attended by a crowd of courtiers.
Order, which the royal ceremonial represents, is breaking down. It is a
mid-speech entry, on the move, by a side door (L). Claudius is at work,
quizzing his spies over Hamlet's behaviour. Rosencrantz and Guildenstern, once milked of their information, are dismissed L. Gertrude
is sent in the same direction after a brief comment to Ophelia, the
second boy actor in the cast, while the three remaining characters
arrange themselves for the next espial. Ophelia, after getting an honest
word of hope from Gertrude that the ploy will come to good, is set
with her book (by standard symbolism a bible or more likely a smaller
book of prayer, emblem of purity) to walk in actorly manner across the
side of the stage (L), while Polonius moves back to the arras (the stage
hangings), waiting for Claudius to join him there. As he walks back to
the arras,[17] Claudius breaks into his first admission that the ghost's
word is true. He pauses, delivering his momentary aside to the yard,
before joining Polonius to stand behind the curtain as Hamlet enters
R, by the door he went through at the end of the last scene.

Hamlet enters speaking to himself. For this soliloquy he holds a
rather different pose from his last, when he was unpacking his heart to
the audience. The 'To be or not to be' speech is more meditative, not
spoken directly to the audience on the side he had entered by, as his
previous soliloquy was. It is not a complaint like the others but a
consideration of the different physical actions now open to him, an
assessment not, as before, of griefs from the past but of courses for the
future. His own hidden passion was voiced to the audience in
the previous soliloquy. Now he meditates on action. The fact that

the audience knows other characters are in earshot affects the speech as a direct communication to them. It is not like the others. He is talking to himself, not to the observers from the metatheatrical world.

He keeps to his side of the stage post while Ophelia walks on the far side of the stage. She must know he is there, since she knows why she has been 'loosed' to him, but pretends to study her book until he hails her. He does so, aptly, when in his soliloquy he comes to the word 'action', the noun that fits both his labour of revenge and the game of false pretences and play-acting that the scene embodies. He renews the pretence, calling her 'Nymph', but she carefully chooses the word Gertrude had left her with, 'Honor'. She, the smaller of the two chief boy actors, approaches awkwardly, stumbling far less artfully than Hamlet into her set speech about having 'longed long' to return his love-tokens. They are wrapped in a small fabric package, which she extends to him with a brief curtsey, but which he rejects with a casual wave. That stimulates a stronger speech from her, ending in a rhyme and the gesture 'There my Lord', offering the packet again with a second, more insistent curtsey, which he reacts against more violently.

By now they are close to each other at the stage front, she keeping her head bowed, he glaring at her for her play-acting. She clings to her part: 'Could beauty, my lord, have better commerce than with honesty?',[18] an honest answer that prompts him to a still louder reaction, ending challengingly, 'I did love you once'. Her response to that prompts (we use these acting terms advisedly) an even more strident reply. It ends in a direct contradiction of his last statement, drawing the most honest words Ophelia could say, 'I was the more deceived'. That stimulates his 'Nunnery' speech, a loud rant ending in the words 'Where's your father?' which have prompted many critics to assume that Hamlet has just seen a movement in the curtains. That is unnecessary, although Polonius and Claudius could have made their presence known to the audience, and to Hamlet if he chose to look towards the *frons*. The exchange between Ophelia and Hamlet took place where the players are in De Witt's drawing of the Swan's stage, so the cloth of arras was at some remove from them. A touch of clowning in the hard-of-hearing *senex* role by Polonius, straining to catch the words by poking his head out through the hangings, is not inconceivable.

Ophelia's reply to Hamlet that her father is at home is her first lie, since she knows all about the plan to eavesdrop on their talk, having been present when Claudius told it to Gertrude. Hamlet's 'Farewell' to her is dismissive, and he starts to leave. She would then properly (and ironically, since she has started lying) fall on her knees to pray for him at that point. Such a pose suits Hamlet's diatribe on his return, since to kneel offers a pert reminder both of Christian truth and of a wedding ceremony. As she prays, he darts about the stage, twice going to the door (R) then back again to where she kneels in the centre front of the platform. His last line, 'To a Nunnery, go' is shouted from the door as he makes his final exit.

Claudius and Polonius re-enter through the arras while she is still on her knees. They ignore her while they analyse Hamlet's behaviour, except for Polonius's brief acknowledgement to his daughter—'How now *Ophelia*? | You neede not tell us, what Lord *Hamlet* saide, | We heard it all'. Status-conscious Polonius still calls Hamlet 'Lord' even after listening to his raving. The two plotters march off L, followed by the weeping boy/girl.

Act 3 scene 2 begins with what must have seemed a grand comic irrelevance to most of the first audiences. There was a fine in-joke in having Burbage as Hamlet lecture his fellow-players about their acting. This ranting prose would have sounded more like a sermon than the eloquent verse of the soliloquies, or the Player King's recital. It has a fine resonance set against the previous scene, where Ophelia's forced untruth about her father is belied by her tears. She cannot act or 'counterfeit' well in the way that everyone else around her is now doing. When Hamlet emphasizes the importance of acting well, he is indirectly confirming his conversion to the importance of seeming over true feeling. How seriously anyone was expected to take this princely amateur's lecture to the professionals about their business depends on how metatheatrically-minded they were.

The scene starts as a mid-speech entry by a small group through door R. Hamlet's role with the players is to act as chamberlain and censor, the presenter of his own show for the royal family. It is in this capacity that he later responds to the worried Claudius's demand 'Have you heard the Argument, is there no Offence in't?' Here he shows the familiarity with the players that signals his having rehearsed them in his lines. These instructions are his final polish. He sends them back again off R to prepare, as Polonius and the other two spies enter L. As compère, he sends the three gentlemen off R after the players, as Horatio enters L. This entry from the inner court marks Horatio's conversion from being a distant student to an intimate of Gertrude and the court, and later shepherd to the mad Ophelia. Here he is Hamlet's confidant, having learned the ghost's story from Hamlet at some off-stage point during Act 2. Now Hamlet needs his own spies, and Horatio will serve. For all Hamlet's declarations of intimate friendship Horatio keeps decorum in calling him 'my Lord', a useful means of continuing to indicate the hero's truly solitary status in the court.

The loud music of drums and trumpets, the instruments normally used for armies to communicate on the battlefield, here marking Claudius's command of Danish power, signals the king's arrival. The stage attendants bring on the royal dais and thrones for Claudius and Gertrude, and the royal procession follows. But this disposition is different. Whereas in the earlier scenes the dais was positioned over the trap, with the royal couple facing the yard, this time they sit facing the *frons*, with the courtiers standing at front stage behind them, facing back towards the *frons*.[19] Now it is the stage-players who have the authority position at the *frons*, using the arras for their entrances, while Claudius is set on the *platea*, the area where carnival and disruption occur. In the earlier scenes set in the royal presence chamber the thrones were backed by the authority of the lords in their balcony rooms on the *frons*; now the lords can see Claudius's face as he prepares to watch the Mousetrap.

The royal entry is as ceremonial as before, but now it is to be the occasion for carnival, marked by the reversed placing of the royal dais. The court groups itself for a festive entertainment. The soldiers escorting Claudius carry torches, to signify that the play is staged at night. The stage attendants bring cushions for the courtiers to sit on. Hamlet tells Horatio to 'Get you a place', and he moves to set himself alongside a stage post opposite Horatio. The king addresses Hamlet courteously, as the most eminent courtier present and his declared son, but Hamlet responds rudely, and still more offensively he turns abruptly away from the throne to speak to Polonius.

There are several metatheatrical exchanges in the dialogue between Polonius and Hamlet. Polonius's story that he played Julius Caesar and was killed by Brutus was an obvious in-joke, since everyone familiar with the Globe would have remembered the player of Polonius taking the title role in the previous year's play, and would know that the player now acting Hamlet had acted Brutus. They were not yet to know that Hamlet/Brutus was to kill Polonius/Caesar again in the next scene of this play. First Rosencrantz reports to compère Hamlet that the players are ready, then Hamlet rejects his mother's invitation to sit on the dais with her and picks out the wan Ophelia. They sit by the other stage post from Horatio's, on the outer side, facing the hangings through which the players enter for their dumbshow once the off-stage hautboys have played to signal their readiness. She sits on a cushion, he on the floor at her feet, as his bawdy offer to lie in her lap indicates.

The hangings are drawn back, to show the players and the '*Banke of Flowers*' before which the events of the dumbshow take place. The players are dressed in worn versions of royal dress, the king with a cardboard crown painted gold. All of them wear wigs. The whole performance of the 'Mousetrap' shows the players in stylized postures which affect Hamlet's attitude to them deeply. His alienation starts with their opening mime. Dumbshows themselves were not as old-fashioned in plays at the time of *Hamlet*'s first staging as has sometimes been claimed, but to mime the story of the play in a preliminary dumbshow was. Certainly Hamlet did not expect it.

The continuing puzzle about the dumbshow is how Claudius fails to be moved by it. He makes no comment, and yet if he sees it he could hardly find it as 'inexplicable' as Ophelia does. He presumably does not watch it, concentrating instead on Gertrude alongside him, something the lords on the stage balcony would be able to note more readily than the groundlings behind his back. Ignoring the play was a lordly form of behaviour not unknown to the occupants of the lords' rooms, who are recorded by different commentators as talking, smoking, and even playing cards during the play. The real audience at the Globe of course had to see it, since the play whose story it summarizes will not be complete when Hamlet interrupts it. At this point, though, Hamlet is worried that his trap will be sprung too soon by the uncomprehending players, either through their dumbshow (which his curses acknowledge as a danger now past), or through the explicitness of the prologue: 'The Players cannot keepe counsell, they'l tell all'. But the

Prologue is innocuous, so Hamlet settles back to his savage jibes at Ophelia. She sits by the post as the target he can attack instead of his mother. As he speaks, he looks across at the occupants of the thrones over the head of Ophelia sitting beside him, to show that the sexual charges are really aimed at Gertrude. She is the only other woman on stage, since the player queen has already been shown to be a boy now almost too tall to play a woman's part.

Hamlet remains motionless until the players have gone back through the arras and Ophelia asks her innocent question about their meaning. His furious replies to her resound through the auditorium, with all the court visibly pretending not to hear them. The same careful silence meets his comment 'Wormwood, Wormwood', as the players present their parody of the queen's protestations of loyalty to her husband even beyond death. Hamlet is following Polonius's advice to Reynaldo, to 'By indirections find directions out', and is camouflaging his real design, lulling Claudius by feigning an attack on Gertrude. His bawdy jibes at Ophelia are to some extent a part of that deception. It is when he challenges Gertrude about what she has heard and she responds modestly that the lady is overstating her case, that Claudius, uncomfortable on his new wife's behalf, intervenes to ask if Hamlet has done his censor's job and checked to ensure that there is no 'offence' in the play's story. Since Hamlet has just that moment applied the story to the queen's remarriage by claiming that she will, unlike Gertrude, keep her vow, Claudius has good reason to question the play's censor.

Hamlet's tension makes him gabble on, even after the murderer has entered to resume the play. He ends his loud and lordly commentary with a neat game of extra application, telling Claudius that the murderer is not brother to the king, but his nephew. Since Claudius was brother to the murdered King Hamlet, the murderer cannot fit Claudius's version of the truth. The nephew to King Claudius, of course, is young Hamlet. He turns a disavowal of the story's application into a concealed threat. When Claudius finally admits that the story does apply to him, he scrambles to his feet, storms forward towards the players and sweeps past them out through the central opening, the players and their flowered bank hastily giving him way. As he strides past them all the courtiers start to their feet in a confused and undignified scramble. Gertrude and the rout of courtiers hasten after him, sweeping with them the still bemused Ophelia, and the guards with their torches, who close the hangings behind them. The empty chair of state and the cushions on which the courtiers sat, left scattered near the stage posts, remain as a mute mark of the violence with which this court scene has dissolved.

This rush of mass movement leaves the space to Hamlet and Horatio, who stood like everyone else when Claudius rose, but remained standing by their posts while everyone else scurried off-stage. The scatter of cushions and empty seats highlight the sudden disorder that Hamlet's play has brought into Denmark. The two men stand looking at each other, the one exultant, vibrating with excitement and bursting with manic play-acting words, the other drily laconic and motionless. Hamlet's gyrations move him towards Horatio at front-stage, though still apart. When he sees Rosencrantz and Guildenstern re-enter through the hangings and approach him he calls for the off-stage musicians. His exchanges with his fellow-students are in quick, excited prose, first one and then the other trying to calm him. When a musician enters R with a recorder, Hamlet gestures the man to approach him and takes it. Guildenstern makes the mistake of using terms that Hamlet had already employed to Horatio, as he makes the courtier's respectful excuse: 'O my Lord, if my Dutie be too bold, my love is too unmannerly.' So Hamlet traps him with the challenge to perform on the musical instrument like a true player. With Polonius, who enters L with the order from Gertrude, he is less patient. He dismisses them all, including Horatio, with a gesture, emphasizing his isolation by lumping them all together as 'Friends', to prepare for his next 'indirection', confronting his mother in answer to her summons. They all exit L, shepherded off by Hamlet.

As he exits L after them, Claudius hurries in R to the still-disordered throne room, followed by the two student spies, breathless from their previous exit through the other door, but obsequious as ever. He sends them off again L, as Polonius enters R, to announce his plan for the next attempt to spy on Hamlet. When he goes off R Claudius, for the first time alone on stage, recounts his guilt to the audience. He strides up and down, canvassing the words he might put into a prayer, before falling on his knees ('Bow stubborne knees') in front of the dais on which his throne stands, facing it and the yard beyond for a last attempt at asking for divine forgiveness in silent prayer. Hamlet enters L, and moves up behind him, drawing his sword and aiming it at Claudius's back until his own words make him pause. He points the sword towards Claudius until he has debated the matter for twelve lines, till he decides 'Up Sword, and know thou a more horrid hent When he is drunke asleepe: or in his Rage, Or in th'incestuous pleasure of his bed', and returns it to its scabbard. He exits L. Claudius then rises slowly, still facing the yard, and speaks his summary couplet before he turns to exit R. The stage hands enter to clear the stage of the royal thrones, carrying them off on their dais through the hangings. The location is visibly changed to Gertrude's private chamber.

Gertrude enters L, followed by Polonius in full flow. Hamlet's voice calls from door L, and Polonius once again conceals himself behind the hangings that cover the central opening. Gertrude speaks firmly to her son, but he grasps her arms to make her kneel on one of the abandoned cushions and listen to him. She, fearing violence from his madness, screams for help. Polonius behind the arras repeats her cries, and Hamlet, once again unsheathing his rapier, runs it through the hangings. Polonius cries out, and is heard to fall heavily. Hamlet, asking hopefully 'is it the King?', draws back the hangings to reveal the corpse. Having identified who it is, he turns his attention entirely to his mother, standing over her ranting as she droops on her cushion. Polonius's corpse lies in the opening of the hangings, so that when the ghost enters he has to step past the corpse. For this third appearance he is dressed (according to Q1) '*in his night gowne*'. There is a fine incongruity in this presentation of the dead husband dressed for his wife's bedchamber, stepping over a corpse as he enters and ignoring it entirely. His use here of the central opening, which he also uses for his exit ('out at the Portall'), reflects his kingly status, while his nightgown reflects the room he is in. The oddity of a domestic scene marked by a corpse in the doorway is of a piece with the fact that the wife cannot see or hear her husband.

Hamlet leaves through the drawn-back curtains of the central opening, going to the body of Polonius to drag the corpse behind him (the F stage direction changes Hamlet's own verb 'lug' for his action to '*tug*'). After taking up the legs of the corpse, he closes the hangings behind him.

e. Act 4

The fourth act flows straight out of the ending of the climax in Act 3 and Hamlet's departure with the corpse, his new affliction. In strict terms this new act is not even marked as a scene break since Gertrude is still on stage after Hamlet leaves to receive Claudius. Editors have marked this as the beginning of Act 4 ever since the 1676 Quarto, with no justification either from the play's structure or its scene breaks. If there was any concept of act divisions, Act 4 would more properly have begun at the end of the previous scene, when the stage hands removed the dais and its thrones. As before, we follow here the traditional editorial division for convenience of reference to the existing editions of the play.

Claudius hurries in R to Gertrude. He is trailed by his new servants, Rosencrantz and Guildenstern, already designated as Hamlet's escorts and captors for his exile in England, now his false friends. Gertrude, still weeping, rises from her cushion as they enter and rush to her. The queen's reaction to Claudius's urgent enquiry, ironic after Hamlet's invocation to repel her new husband, is that she must tell him in private. She sends the two students off R, while she gives Claudius a part-explanation of her grief. All she can do is insist that it was a fit of madness that made Hamlet kill Polonius, adding the obviously false claim that he left in tears over what he had done. Claudius summons the students back from door R and sends them off L to find Hamlet and the corpse. He helps Gertrude off R.

Hamlet enters for the next scene through the hangings, where he had exited with the corpse. He is hardly on stage before the loud voices of Rosencrantz and Guildenstern precede their breathless entry L with soldiers. Neither the students nor the soldiers, who are clothed like Barnardo and Francisco in the opening scenes, are now his friends. They surround him, the soldiers holding their halberds nervously on guard. When he orders them to take him to the king, the students lead off L, followed by Hamlet with the soldiers behind him. Claudius enters R, with two courtiers and two stage hands, who stand by the doors. F is usually more economical with walk-on parts than Q2, as if the text's passage through the playhouse routinely trimmed the number of players. Here, though, a large body of support for the oppressed king ought to have been essential. The next scene, requiring Fortinbras with his army, may have forced a cut in the numbers for this scene. Rosencrantz enters L, to announce that Hamlet is under guard, and Hamlet is then brought in by Guildenstern and the soldiers. When Claudius demands to know where the body is, Hamlet gestures to the stage cover, as the emblem of heaven, and to the trap, as hell. He has already gestured once before in the presence of the two students to the stage's heavenly canopy. Now, having become a murderer, he can add its opposite. His third alternative is indicated with a gesture to the *frons*, where he lugged the body off at the end of the previous scene. Claudius sends the stage-hands off through the hangings to find the body. Hamlet leaves L, escorted by the soldiers, and Claudius sends Rosencrantz and Guildenstern after him, urging speed. He stays behind to tell the audience of his further plot, and leaves L after the others.

The next scene, 4.4, lengthy in Q2 but reduced to ten lines in F, is where Fortinbras makes his first appearance, asking permission to march over Danish soil. It was necessary to register Fortinbras as a presence before his arrival at the finale, but in the F version Hamlet's soliloquy was cut to speed the staging, and the scene reduced to a minimum without Hamlet appearing at all.[20] The irrelevance and imprecision of the information given in the soliloquy together with its absence from the Folio has led many critics to see it as a speech that was never fitted properly into the text. In the shorter version, Fortinbras enters R '*with an Armie*', consisting of a captain, an ensign carrying a banner, a drummer, and two soldiers with halberds. Fortinbras is dressed like a general, in similar armour to the ghost of King Hamlet on its first appearance, and similarly carrying a marshal's baton or 'truncheon'. The dead king's soldierly look in 1.2 contrasted strongly with the look of studious and black-clad Hamlet, and so does the martial appearance of Fortinbras here. Acting formally, as a general, he marches to centre stage before ordering his captain to go ahead towards the court to request leave for the march over Danish soil.[21] The captain leaves L, followed by Fortinbras at the head of the soldiers.

The original version (Q2) opened with the strange general leading his army on-stage R to a drumbeat, marching round the stage ('*over the stage*'), before halting at the front. The army marched to the drumbeat, following the fully armoured Fortinbras with his truncheon.

Fortinbras ordered the captain to go to the Danish king, and led his army off L. The captain walked back towards the other door as Hamlet entered with his escort from the door R which the army had entered by. Hamlet stopped him to ask about the army he had just seen marching off the stage.[22] Once he had given his answer, the captain exited R. Hamlet sent Rosencrantz and Guildenstern off L ahead of him, remaining to speak his final soliloquy of self-laceration to the audience. He then exited L after his escort.

The rest of what editors call Act 4 is concerned through a rapid sequence of comings and goings with the consequences of Hamlet murdering Polonius. First Gertrude enters R, escorted by a gentleman for the scene following the culprit's departure. F cuts the gentleman, and like Q1 gives this set of speeches to Horatio, which may be correct, although it changes his role from visitor to the court into an intimate. He is not named in Q2 after the initial stage direction. To make him the gentleman would have been an obvious economy in casting.

Gertrude enters in mid-speech, refusing to give an audience to Ophelia because she herself is still distraught from the disaster. Her escort uses Hamlet's word, 'distract', to describe Ophelia's state of mind. Hamlet had first applied it to the globe and the Globe. Subsequently Rosencrantz reported to Claudius that Hamlet had called himself distracted. Later, Claudius applies the same term to the 'multitude' who love Hamlet. In his apology to Laertes, Hamlet himself will claim to have been punished with 'a sore distraction'. Here the word signals how Ophelia now suffers in truth what Hamlet's 'antic disposition' has allowed him to enact in counterfeit.

As the gentleman (in the Folio version Horatio) brings her in by door R to speak to Gertrude, the queen at front stage delivers a four-line statement to the audience about her 'sick soule' and her 'guilt' over her lechery and incest. That brief comment, so similar to the first confession by Claudius, registers the impact Hamlet's diatribe has had on her, and her lack of self-control. She cannot face Ophelia, the victim of her son's madness, for which her sins make her responsible.[23] So her misery prepares us for the sight of '*Ophelia distracted*', as the Folio has it.

Traditionally madness in women was marked by a long wig of loose hair. If Q1's stage direction is to be trusted, he/she also carried a lute, to accompany herself when she sang. It has been argued, by Harold

Jenkins for instance (ed. *Hamlet*, p. 348), that since the snatches of ballads form part of the dialogue, she would not have needed the lute, and that it is an actor's embellishment. Whoever thought of it first, the Q1 stage direction does indicate that it became a tradition in the staging very early.

Ophelia's lines are brief prose introductions to her ballad stanzas: 'Pray you marke', she says as she launches in her boy's alto or treble into another bawdy ballad rhyme. She perambulates around the stage in short, stabbing steps while she speaks and sings, moving to stare into one face after another, first at Gertrude, then at Claudius, and then off on her own, while the others confer anxiously behind her. She exits L, followed by the gentleman who had escorted her in, and then at Claudius's urging by the second gentleman (Horatio).

As Horatio goes to the door Claudius tells Gertrude that this madness of Ophelia's is true grief, unlike Hamlet's, and continues to hint that the blame lies with her son. He announces Laertes's return from Paris in secret, just as the noises off give warning of his arrival. The 'Messenger' who enters R to warn Claudius is so named in Q2 and F because he is neither a gentleman nor a soldier (his dress is actually that of a stage hand). He is clearly not one of the royal household's Swiss guards, whom Claudius summons when he sees that the stage hand is unarmed. Laertes, sword in hand, followed by a group of working men in jerkins carrying cudgels, enters after him R. Laertes sends them out again, telling the last to guard the door from outside. The man closes it behind him, leaving Laertes to advance to where the king and Gertrude stand by a stage post. He stands in front of Claudius, not kneeling to him, sword poised, and Gertrude takes his left arm to restrain him. Laertes stands still with her hand on his arm until Claudius instructs her to release him. Claudius reassures Gertrude with a regal gesture ('Do not feare our person'), and draws Laertes from the repetition of his curt demand 'Where's my Father?' into a longer speech, the first sign of his cooling. Claudius soothes him, turning his anger away from its immediate target, and is winning his way into rational speech when Ophelia is heard off-stage through the closed door R, and the king orders the door to be opened so that she can enter.

The signs of her madness are immediately recognizable to Laertes. His curt fury turns to words of grief, commenting on her snatches of song and her words as she walks round the characters on stage as before, handing out herbs to each one she passes. The rosemary for remembrance and the pansies she gives to Laertes, the fennel and columbines to Gertude, and the rue to Claudius, holding some back for herself. The daisy also goes to the king.[24] After her last song she exits quickly R with a Christian farewell. Claudius holds Laertes back, drawing him to the side of the stage where a stage post conceals them from Gertrude to draw him into his commitment to revenge. Claudius summons Gertrude to go with them as they all exit R.

Horatio enters L followed by a stage hand dressed in servant's blue, to hear about the seamen and their message. The servant goes off L, and a man dressed in seamen's slops (jerkin and baggy Dutch breeches) enters with Hamlet's letter. When Horatio has read it aloud, they both exit hastily L, Horatio going first. As they leave, Claudius enters R followed by Laertes. They resume the exchange that Claudius began after Ophelia's exit as they walk together to centre stage, the king giving a reason for his inaction. He is preparing to say how he has dealt with Hamlet in England when a servant enters L with two papers, one of which he gives to Claudius. Claudius takes it, breaks the seal and reads it silently. He looks up, dismisses the servant who has backed to the door L, and reads it aloud to Laertes. They walk forward, Laertes gesturing excitedly as they develop their plot, Claudius more controlled and cool. He watches Laertes carefully as he describes the French gallant, turning away when he comes to Hamlet's envy at the account of Laertes's skill as a swordsman, then facing him abruptly as he questions his sincerity, in a phrase 'the painting of a sorrow', ironically repeating Hamlet's contempt for seeming expressed in the play's second scene.

This is a scene in which the body movement of the two men is as contrastive as their speech. Young Laertes is excited, agitated, sudden and violent in movement, striding across the front of the stage while he speaks. Claudius stands still nearer centre stage, regal in his dress and his pose, but much more obviously the actor, adopting poses to persuade and manipulate the younger man. His sudden switches of tone—from flattery to '*Laertes* was your Father deare to you?', from planning a killing to the false piety of 'No place indeed should murder Sanctuarize'—emphasize his dissembling as opposed to the more honest emotion of the other. As the plot develops, their body language gradually reverses. Claudius's regal pose slips, and his speech becomes more open and excited as Laertes's overt emotion slips into a more passive acquiescence. By the time he comes to the poison that they will use 'If he by chance escape your venom'd stuck', they are united in the pleasure their plot gives them.

They conclude their plot at front stage, by the groundlings. Gertrude's entry L suddenly breaks in on their intimacy. She starts to tell her story breathlessly as she hurries from the *frons* towards them. She comes to a stop at the shocking word 'drown'd', in mid-stage, and stands still, taking a long breath to go on with her eloquent tale. Laertes covers his face, then forbids his tears and rushes past Gertrude and out L. Claudius follows him, gathering Gertrude with his arm and speaking to her urgently as they hurry after him.

f. Act 5

The 'two Clownes' enter R (see Fig. 4), to an immediate lightening of the mood. The first with a mattock, the second carrying a spade, they move forward and open the trapdoor in the centre of the stage. The lead clown stands waist-high inside the trap with the mattock ('Goodman Delver') while he quizzes the other, who serves as his comic feed, holding the spade until the Gravedigger asks for it.[25] For all the lightness, the gravedigger begins with a direct reference to the question whether the self-drowned Ophelia, whose last words were a wish for God's mercy on 'all Christian Soules', should have a Christian burial. Their comic dialogue comes to an end as Hamlet and Horatio enter L, staying '*afarre off*' and walking slowly up the side of the stage.[26] The Gravedigger sends his feed off R, and while the gravedigger digs and sings Hamlet and Horatio slowly draw nearer. They speak prose, informally, to signal the casualness of their talk. Hamlet's comment on the singer's lack of respect for his job comes between the clown's stanzas.

While singing the second stanza the clown picks up a skull from inside the trap and places it on the stage alongside him. It evokes Hamlet's comment that the tongue inside the skull could also sing once. His comment on the way the clown handled it is the kind of explanatory note that Shakespeare often used to accompany an action that might not be visible to all the audience. That would be the case if

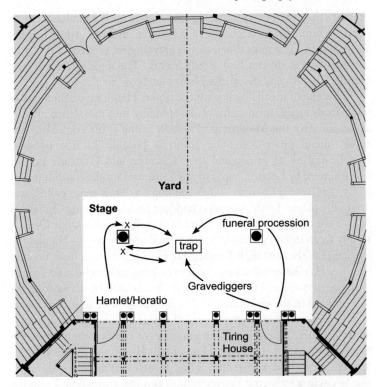

Figure 4. (Detail of Figure 2.) *Hamlet*, 5.1. The chief moves are (*a*) the two gravediggers enter R, and move to the trapdoor in the centre of the stage; (*b*) Hamlet and Horatio enter L, and walk forward to the nearer stage post, where they stand 'aloof' before joining the gravedigger at the trap; (*c*) the funeral procession enters R, and processes round the stage to the front centre, where they turn to the trap. Hamlet and Horatio withdraw to the left, by the stage post, until Hamlet plunges forward to fight Laertes in the trap.

Hamlet and Horatio had by then approached close enough to the trap to obscure the digger from some of the audience behind them. They continue their conversation, however, as if they were still not close enough for him to hear them. He must continue working, throwing up a second skull which Hamlet also comments on. For them to speak as if he were not there was another mark of the differences in their status. They acknowledge consistently the different social grades of the three present, the two gentry ignoring the clown until Hamlet turns to question him. Horatio regularly calls Hamlet 'my Lord', while Hamlet according to Q2 speaks down to the gravedigger as 'sirrah'. In Q1 he patronizingly addresses him as 'my friend'. The digger, not knowing Hamlet's identity, acknowledges him merely as 'Sir'.

By the end of the dialogue with the clown, Hamlet is on the verge of self-parody again, turning his philosophizing into moralizing rhyme, as he did after the Mousetrap. This idle game is interrupted by the royal funeral procession. The coffin is brought in first by door R, followed by its priest, and then Claudius and Gertrude side by side followed by Laertes, and lastly by Osric and another lord. It is very likely that 'young Ostricke' (Q2's spelling), as he is twice called, was originally played by the boy who had just finished playing Ophelia.[27] All we see of Ophelia herself here is the coffin. In this scene Osric is simply an attendant gentleman, not named until he brings Hamlet the challenge to the duel with Laertes. He must be on stage here, because he notes Hamlet's misleading claim to be king, a claim he makes much of in the next scene. His identity might be clarified by his wearing for this procession the elaborate hat that he was to flourish in that scene.

The royal entrants progress round the edge of the stage on the right, while Hamlet, Horatio and the gravedigger hastily retreat from the trap behind the left stage post. Hamlet tells Horatio to step 'aside', and 'Couch we awhile, and mark'. They crouch behind the stage post, slowly circling to keep it between them and the procession. From the other side the procession moves round the stage post and reaches the centre front, turning towards the *frons* and going as far as the grave-trap, where it halts. Hamlet and Horatio, behind their stage post, are then on the yard side of the funeral group. The coffin is set down across the stage on the yard side. The priest stands by it on the *frons* side facing the yard, the others lining up on each side of the trap facing inwards, on the inner side of the stage posts. Laertes, standing across the coffin from the priest, his back to the yard, makes the same kind of curt demand of the priest that he had made of Claudius. It is on his orders not the priest's that the coffin is laid inside the trap, and it is Gertrude not the priest who strews flowers on the coffin. Laertes goes further, leaping into the trap himself and shouting to the gravedigger to conclude the ceremony by heaping earth on both the living and the dead. His verb, when he says 'now *pile* your dust, upon the quick and dead', indicates that he is ordering the gravedigger, not the priest, to finish the burial. After addressing the body, he turns to the clown with his order to 'Hold off the earth a while', then orders him to cover both with his spade.

It is at this point that Hamlet springs forward from behind the stage post to offer what is probably his most misunderstood piece of play acting. Like Henry V's killing of the French prisoners at Agincourt which Gower misinterprets on stage (an on-stage character's misreading followed by most productions through the centuries), the reading which the stage audience here, and especially the courtier Osric, gives to Hamlet's act has been followed by centuries of editors. Osric hears Hamlet declare that he is the king of Denmark, and in the next scene behaves accordingly. In fact the trap as a grave reminds Hamlet of his own previous encounters with the trap, when the ghost of his dead father appeared through it. Hysterically, he parodies his father's own advent with the histrionic declaration 'This is I, *Hamlet* the Dane!' 'The Dane' was the king of Denmark. Hamlet plays his dead father the king returning from the place of the dead. It is another of his impersonations, his play-acting, but it is one that nobody on stage, other than Horatio, can possibly understand. The accident that the new actor of the ghostly role shares his name with the dead figure he is impersonating ensures that the viewers assume that he is mad, and that ambition has deluded him into thinking he is the king. His leap into the trap to grapple with Laertes, as we are told by the Q1 stage direction, '*Hamlet leapes in after Leartes* [sic]', along with other signals he gives them, confirms their assumption that he is mad and deluded. To the symbol-conscious Elizabethan audience, however, jumping into the trap also confirmed Hamlet's readiness to enter hell like Laertes in pursuit of his revenge. Revengers paid the price of damnation for the blood they drew.

A slightly longer-term view of this union of the two in battle inside the trap affirms their equivalence as would-be revengers of the murders of their two fathers. Hamlet is the target for Laertes' revenge, Laertes the surrogate for Hamlet's. Like the subsequent duel in the finale, this equivalence registers Hamlet's view of his conflict as ideally a noble and open duel, the kind of confrontation which killed Rosencrantz and Guildenstern when they were caught between the swords of the two 'mighty opposites'.

In a more private way the struggle with Laertes offers Hamlet a characteristically oblique means of registering his reaction to the news of Ophelia's death. He joins the brother and sister in hell, three victims of parental murders, two of them fatal revengers.[28] That equivalence becomes more direct when Hamlet challenges Laertes to enact his grief in words, in the self-consciously exhibitionistic speech which he ends by acknowledging the falsification inherent in the words of passion: 'Nay, an thou'lt mouth, Ile rant as well as thou.' As he exits L he returns to the reality of action with his last and most dismissive reference to Hercules. Claudius sends Horatio after him, and turns to Laertes to renew the promise in their plot before leading the funeral group off R.

The final scene of the play begins with Hamlet entering in mid-conversation with Horatio (see Fig. 5). They enter L, the door they left by, and proceed around the flanks of the stage as they talk. Both are wearing their hats and their gentlemanly rapiers. Their forms of address ('Sir' and 'my Lord') renew their social distance, which para-doxically affirms their closeness, although they grow more intimate as the subject gets hotter. Osric, recognizable from the graveside scene, enters to them R. He doffs his hat to them. The Q2 spelling 'Ostricke' may indicate that his hat should have been decorated with that supreme ornament of late Elizabethan gallantry, an ostrich feather. He makes a gracious arms-length gesture with it, and waits at a respectful distance while they turn their backs to exchange what they know of him. When they turn to him again he commences his speech, clasping his hat to his breast. He has heard Hamlet call himself the King of Denmark, as he thinks, and so he follows the decorum proper to addressing an authority figure, and keeps his hat in his hand. This irritates Hamlet, who expects the more normal behaviour between gentlemen, which would require Osric to put his hat back on as Hamlet has just done after the greeting, and urges him to do so. Osric, knowing that mad Hamlet thinks himself to be the king, is determined to humour his madness and behave to him as if he were king, so twice refuses to obey Hamlet's urging. Hamlet parodies his language, which he sees as consistent in its falsity with his excessively obsequious behaviour. Osric returns his hat to his head only as he covers the distance from front stage to his exit at door R, evoking Horatio's comment about the proverb of the lapwing chick leaving the nest with the eggshell still on his feathered head.

The rest of the scene begins slowly and formally, developing a faster
and faster pace as it moves into violent and uncontrolled action. In
what was probably the original text, Q2, a lord enters by the same door
R as Osric left by, to ask if Hamlet is ready for the duel. F and Q1 cut
this brief entry. Hamlet and Horatio remain at the stage front for their
last conversation, until two stage hands part the hangings to admit the
royal party through the central opening. First a table is brought on
stage, and placed in the centre over the trap, a little behind the line of
the stage posts. The royal dais is placed behind it, nearer the *frons* and
facing the yard, and after a trumpet-call Claudius and Gertrude enter
and take their seats, followed by the whole cast, who arrange themselves around the dais across the *frons* behind the thrones, sitting on
the cushions the stage attendants bring them. Beside one of the
flanking doors an attendant stands holding a tray with two flagons of
wine. Through the other door Osric leads in two servants who carry
the swords, daggers, and gauntlets for the duel, wrapped in rich cloth.
They stand to one side of the royal dais, facing the centre by the table
in front of Claudius. Laertes stands on the other side of the table, while
Hamlet and Horatio continue to stand at the stage edge watching
them all.[29]

Claudius rises and summons Hamlet to approach the table. He
takes Laertes's hand and puts it into Hamlet's. Still holding it, Hamlet
makes his elaborate speech of apology to Laertes, an oblique claim that
madness is not Hamlet's true self, and that he is now no longer mad.
Laertes accepts the apology stiffly, releasing his hand as he says 'I stand
aloofe'. Consequently Hamlet's 'embrace' is metaphorical. It is mildly
ironic that the duel, the only possible confrontation with Claudius that
Hamlet had considered earlier in his talk with Horatio, the 'fell
incensed swords of mighty opposites', should now appear as a pretend
duel with a substitute antagonist.

The stage movements are swift now, formal and economical, revealing the complex interrelations, the secret knowingness and the ignorance of the different participants. Horatio stands ready to back
Hamlet. Laertes shifts uneasily between the king and Osric. Hamlet
turns to the servant holding the foils, but is sidetracked by his own
witplay as 'foil' to Laertes, which lets Osric come forward to control
the issue of the swords. It is to Osric under his elaborately-feathered
hat that Laertes turns to get the lethal replacement for his first choice.

It is possible that changes in the fashion for duelling affected the texts here. F's reference to '*Gauntlets*' in place of Q2's daggers in the entry stage direction has been taken to mean a change in the weaponry used for the duel, at some point between the original composition of Q2 in 1600 or 1601 and the playhouse alteration of F before 1623. In the change, swords and daggers were replaced by swords and gauntlets, to facilitate the grasping of each other's swords in the exchange, where Q1 records '*They catch one anothers Rapiers*'.

Once they have their rapiers, and have taken their places at front-stage, Hamlet on the left and Laertes on the right, Claudius summons the stage attendant to place the goblets on the table in front of him. With eloquent gestures he holds up the poisoned pearl, and orders the on-stage drum to speak to the off-stage trumpet, which instructs a chamber (the firing-piece of a small cannon) to be detonated, as before in 1.4 when Hamlet complained about the Danish court's carousing, from the gable-front of the heavens over the stage.[30] Claudius seats himself behind the table on the right, Gertrude on the left, Hamlet's side. Osric stands with his back to the stage edge as the umpire, his rapier ready.

The duellists stand in their shirts, their doublets off. Hamlet makes himself ready with Horatio's help, Laertes alone on the right. Starting formally, they engage in their first bout, played across the front in a line between the posts and Osric at the stage edge. In the gentlemen's rooms near the stage balcony the skill of their swordsmanship would have found some sharp judges. They could look down on the combat from the upper-gallery level, at a distance of about twenty-five feet, over the heads of the courtiers and Claudius behind the table. The bout is played at some length. In the end Hamlet touches Laertes. Laertes angrily denies it, but Osric judges it a 'palpable hit', and Laertes calls Hamlet to start another bout immediately. Claudius demands that they pause, asks for the goblets, and stands to put the pearl into the left-hand of the two, the side on which Hamlet is standing. Claudius, on the right, drinks from the right-hand cup, tacitly admitting which side he is on. The drum, trumpet, and chamber renew their triumphant noises. He offers the left-hand cup to Hamlet. Hamlet, however, asks for it to be put back on the table until they have fought their second bout. Claudius sits again.

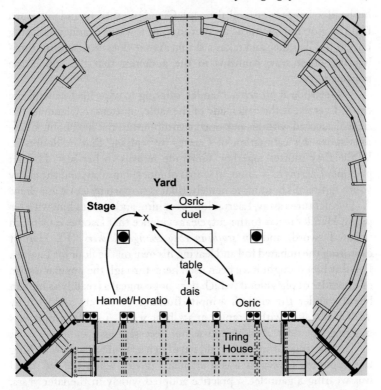

Figure 5. *Hamlet*, 5.2. The chief moves are (*a*) Hamlet and Horatio entering L, and standing by the L stage post, to be joined by Osric entering R, and crossing the stage to talk to them. He leaves them by the same lengthy route. (*b*) For the duel, the royal group are preceded through the central opening by stage-hands bringing on the dais and its thrones, and the table set in front of them. (*c*) The duel takes place with Hamlet L and Laertes R, in front of the table, with Osric standing at the front of the stage.

In the second bout Hamlet again finally catches Laertes with the point of his rapier, and this time Laertes admits it. The pace is quickening. Claudius tells Gertrude loudly that Hamlet will win, and she fondly replies that he is hot and breathless. She stands to offer him a cloth, then taking the goblet from her side of the table holds it up, saying 'The Queene Carowses to thy fortune, *Hamlet*.' It is an entertaining game, and she is backing the winner. Hamlet bends his head to her gesture, and although Claudius exclaims and puts out a hand to stop her she turns away from him towards Hamlet, excusing herself to Claudius, and takes a drink. As she does so Claudius, turning the other way, confirms to the audience that the cup is the poisoned one.

As Gertrude approaches Hamlet, offering to wipe his face with the cloth, Laertes, at the other side of the table, mutters to Claudius that he will succeed with his poisoned swordpoint in the next bout. Claudius shows his estimation of Laertes by replying that he doubts it. While they mutter together, Gertrude returns to her seat. Hamlet prompts Laertes to resume, in words of mock-humility, and the angry youth fights this bout more fiercely, till it is stopped by Osric as a draw. As Hamlet turns away, Laertes lunges at him, and catches him with his point. Hamlet reacts to the cut, clear evidence that Laertes is using an unbated sword, and '*In scuffling they change Rapiers*' (F), Hamlet capturing the unbated foil and leaving his own on the floor for Laertes. Possibly blood might have been used here, through the popular device of a bladder of pig's blood (which does not congeal as readily as human blood), under the victim's armpit. Burbage, however, could hardly display his skill with a rapier at its best while his left armpit was hugging a bladder. Real blood was not necessary just yet.

The exchange of swords would have been a familiar tactic. Catching the opponent's weapon was a standard device when the left hand was wearing a gauntlet, a practice adopted widely in the later years, up to 1620. More rarely, the dagger might be used in rapier and dagger fights to twist the opponent's rapier out of his hand. In this heated instance, F's 'scuffling' suggests a less than orthodox kind of struggle, product of Hamlet's outrage at the trick indicated by the unbated sword.

They renew the fight, ignoring Claudius's disingenuous order to Osric to separate them. Hamlet wounds Laertes with the unbated sword just as Gertrude falls forward, clutching the table. Osric, still trying to act as umpire on the yard side of the stage, between the combatants and facing the table, is the first to see her collapse. As the fight pauses, both stop in their combatant positions in front of the stage posts, perhaps now showing blood on their shirts. Horatio moves to Hamlet and Osric to Laertes to hold them and check their injuries. Laertes admits to Osric the failure of their plot, but Hamlet's concern is all for Gertrude. Claudius, standing helplessly as the others move around him, tries to claim that she is swooning at the sight of blood, but she struggles up from the table, holding a goblet, crying poison as she collapses to the floor by the table.

Hamlet shouts treachery, and orders the door to be locked, to keep everyone on stage. The attendants stand by the doors nonplussed. On the right-hand side Osric leaves Laertes and rushes past the table and the dais to the door R, slipping through and shutting it behind him. Both Q2 and F give the announcement of Fortinbras's arrival later in the scene to Osric. He thus has to exit at some point between his pointing at the collapsing Gertrude and the off-stage drumbeat which announces Fortinbras. Hamlet's order to lock the door has to be acknowledged somehow. Allowing the slippery Osric his escape here seems appropriate as part of the general reaction to the order.

Laertes, now slumped to the floor, distracts attention from Osric's escape by calling out to Hamlet and identifying Claudius as the cause of both the poisoned sword and the drink. Hamlet, still holding the unbated sword, rushes at Claudius behind the table and stabs him. The courtiers scatter, shrieking treason. Claudius calls for help, but they dare not move. Hamlet drops his sword, takes the goblet and, holding Claudius's head, applies it to his mouth. Claudius drinks and dies, and the action begins to slow again. Laertes dies after acknowledging the equivalence of Hamlet's case with his own. Hamlet, still holding the poisoned goblet, kneels, and then slumps on the ground as he asks Horatio to tell his story. He sets the goblet beside him. When Horatio reacts by taking it up Hamlet reaches out to snatch it back, and they struggle over it for a moment, the last of the liquid spilling as Hamlet secures it.

A drumbeat and a cannon (chamber) shot are heard off-stage, and Osric re-enters L to announce the return of Fortinbras. Hamlet dies after giving his vote for the election of the next king to the newcomer. Fortinbras enters L in step with an English ambassador and followed by his army marching with their halberds. He comments on the bodies, to which the ambassador adds the deaths of Rosencrantz and Guildenstern. Horatio gestures to the body of Claudius, saying that it was not he who ordered their deaths. Apart from the newcomer only Horatio and Osric, it seems, are to survive the havoc. It is that which gives the authority role at the end to Horatio, the only informed observer of 'these things', and to Fortinbras, the only avenger of the original three who has not drawn blood in revenge.

The presence of Fortinbras, still in the general's armour of his previous appearance in 4.4, adds several resonances to the close. His military dress makes sense of his order that the funeral procession for Hamlet should be soldierly. He links Hamlet to his own seeming in giving the order that Hamlet should be borne 'like a Soldier' to the 'Stage' for his final action. But in giving this order he makes at least one major and unjustified deduction. Horatio, the insider, has proposed that all of 'these bodies' should be placed high on a stage 'to the view'. Without having heard any details about how Claudius and Gertrude, Hamlet and Laertes were killed, Fortinbras instead orders that only Hamlet should be so honoured. He knows nothing about the 'wounded name' which made Hamlet insist that Horatio told his story to the world. Fortinbras's statement that Hamlet was likely to have proved most royal 'had he beene put on', is patronizing, as if Hamlet was no more than the heir to royal events, and had a potential as a soldier which he had no chance to realize. That alone indicates how little this outsider knows of what has just happened on the stage. Yet he selects Hamlet as the object for a ceremonious military burial ahead of the dead king.

That Fortinbras should give such an unorthodox order may have been meant in part as a reflection on his obtuseness, and yet also his instinct for the truth. His mental and physical difference from Hamlet had been implied throughout. From an initial position as son of the former Norwegian king and the new king's nephew, an exact reflection of Hamlet's own status after his father's death, we know that he started with his 'List of Landlesse Resolutes' to revenge the killing of his father by Hamlet's father using military means. Thwarted in that, he was diverted into trying a military expedition of no material profit. Now he can, with unconscious irony, 'embrace my Fortune' in Denmark.

The '*Peale of Ordenance*' which is fired off-stage while the funeral procession is marching off makes another nicely ironic comment on all the previous cannonfire, each one of which has sounded to celebrate Claudius drinking. The gunfire was first heard while Hamlet was talking bitterly to Horatio about the deep drinking at the Danish court. It sounded again when Claudius was planning to poison Hamlet. Now it sounds to close the play with the military noise that marked a great man's funeral. In the conventional terms of royal ceremonies, it would have been an appropriate sound to mark the death of King Claudius. But the loud noise that Claudius had been accustomed to order as a mark of his carousing now echoes around the auditorium to mark his supplanting by Hamlet. The dead prince, not the king, is given the ceremony fitting for a dead soldier. This final act of seeming at the end is, in its own way, as exhibitionistic and as counterfeit as his continuing to wear the black of mourning for his father at the remarriage of his mother. That he should be treated by the obtuse Fortinbras 'like a soldier' renews the sense of visual counterfeiting and deception that has run throughout the play.

We noted above that the military dress that Fortinbras wore in his two appearances on stage develops a much weightier significance in the finale than the image of another soldier like King Hamlet succeeding to the throne of Denmark instead of young and unmilitary Hamlet. Armoured Fortinbras had a potent influence on how Elizabethans would have read the conclusion. In armour, wearing a helmet with beaver, and carrying a general's truncheon, Fortinbras renews the appearance of the ghost in the first act. All Elizabethan playgoers were familiar with the archetypal revenge tradition in the form of *The Spanish Tragedy*. Its ghost appearing at the beginning and returning at the end exemplified the revenge tradition which would be strong in the minds of the first viewers. They would have expected the vengeful ghost of Act 1 to return at the end to celebrate his victory. A true ghost would certainly have chosen to praise the dead revenger Hamlet rather than the dead king Claudius on whom his vengeance had been enacted. The finale's ghost-like visitor, though, has none of the ghost's knowledge. He is not even a revenger. He does the right thing out of ignorance, and his resemblance to the dead King Hamlet becomes a concluding gambit in the long game of seeming and counterfeiting. His ghostly appearance, when he turns out to be the sole revenger still alive, and alive precisely because he had forsaken his vengeance, is probably the most delicate irony in the whole play. Fortinbras could now grasp more than the material fortune that he started after on his vengeful quest, and take it without having actually to kill anyone. Such a subversion of the traditional revenging ghost leaves the ending in the hands of metatheatre rather than cathartic pity or fear.

g. The Jig as Metatheatre

For the original audiences for *Hamlet* at the Globe there was in all likelihood one further exhibition of the seeming and counterfeiting inherent in playmaking waiting to register in their minds. Thomas Platter reported that when he went to the Globe on 21 September 1599 to see *Julius Caesar*, the performance ended with a jig: 'at the end of the play they danced together admirably and exceedingly gracefully, according to their custom, two in each group dressed in men's and two in women's apparel'.[31] Jigs enacted a short and usually bawdy story, the characters singing their rhyming dialogue to ballad metres as they danced. Most of the surviving jig-stories are not far from being bedroom farce. They went out of favour at the Globe, possibly as early as the time between the first staging of *Julius Caesar* and *Hamlet*, since the company's most eminent jig-maker, Will Kemp, left them late in 1599 to perform his marathon morris-jig to Norwich.[32] The company certainly abandoned jigs after 1609, when they acquired the Blackfriars consort of musicians to entertain the audience during the preliminaries and the interacts to their plays.

Hamlet's contempt for Polonius with his taste for jigs and bawdry may have echoed sentiments already being expressed by members of the company. This switch in tastes, however, was probably not reflected in the first years at the Globe, when the company's traditional offering of a concluding jig after the performance was still part of everyone's expectation. There is something attractive in the idea of a jig concluding this tragedy, just as it concluded the original performances of *Julius Caesar*. While the enactment of Fortinbras accepting the Danish crown as his 'fortune' makes a comment on what Hamlet with his vote expects for Denmark at the end of the play, so a jig would have been a comment on how persistent were the Polonian tastes which Hamlet had thrown such potent scorn at. In its own way, a jig would have put a final gloss on the play's insistence on the performance as metatheatre, the play within the play.

CHAPTER I

1. Quotations from Shakespeare in this book are taken from *Shakespeare's Plays in Quarto: A Facsimile Edition of Copies Mainly from the Henry E. Huntington Library*, ed. Michael J. B. Allen and Kenneth Muir (Berkeley and Los Angeles, 1981), and *The Norton Facsimile: The First Folio of Shakespeare*, ed. Charlton Hinman (2nd edn., New York, 1996). Act, scene and line references are those in *William Shakespeare: The Complete Works*, ed. Stanley Wells and Gary Taylor (Oxford, 1986).

2. See Chapter 5b, 'Siege Scenes'.

3. *Henry V*, Chorus, 4.0.53. The early fashion for plays about English history, and the recurrent insistence on their title-pages that they were telling a 'True History', is one indication of the general unease over staging fictions.

4. At the opening of *Julius Caesar* the tribunes chide the commoners for not carrying their tools. They reply that it is a holiday, a time for discarding their tools (and also the days when artisans were freed to attend plays). The groundlings who were artisans in the handicraft trades must have reacted to this exchange.

5. Thomas Overbury, *Characters*, ed. W. J. Paylor (Oxford, 1936), 41.

6. Everard Guilpin, *Skialetheia*, 1598, Epigram 53.

7. See Fig. 1, De Witt's drawing of the Swan, 1596. De Witt was a Dutch priest on leave in London. He wrote to his friend Arendt van Buchell about his experiences, and van Buchell made copies, including one of his drawing, discovered amongst his papers in the University of Utrecht Library in 1888.

8. See John Orrell, *The Theatres of Inigo Jones and John Webb* (Cambridge, 1985), ch. 3.

9. These are reproduced in, for instance, Andrew Gurr, *The Shakespearean Stage 1574–1642*, 3rd edn. (Cambridge, 1992), 5, 163. See also John H. Astington, 'The Origins of the *Roxana* and *Messallina* Illustrations', *Shakespeare Survey*, 43 (1991), 149–69.

10. See Robert Weimann, *Shakespeare and the Popular Tradition in the Theatre: Studies in the Social Dimension of Dramatic Form and Function*, trans. and ed. Robert Schwartz (Baltimore and London, 1978), ch. 6.

11. T. J. King, *Casting Shakespeare's Plays. London actors and their roles, 1590–1642* (Cambridge, 1992), 199–201.

12. Much of what we know about the day-to-day practices of the companies at this time comes from the notebooks of Philip Henslowe, builder of the Rose. His accounts and contracts with the players and other papers can be found in *Henslowe's Diary*, ed. R. A. Foakes and R. T. Rickert (Cambridge, 1961).

13. See Andrew Gurr, *The Shakespearian Playing Companies* (Oxford, 1996), ch. 4.

14. James Burbage's name 'Theatre' for his 1576 building was an allusion to the Roman theatres, although when he gave it that name a 'Theatre' was normally not thought of as a playhouse but an atlas, a collection of maps. The name chosen in 1599 reflected the original meaning as well as the tag 'Totus mundus agit histrionem' which became the new playhouse's motto. See Richard Dutton, '*Hamlet, An Apology for Actors*, and The Sign of the Globe', *Shakespeare Survey* 41 (1989), 35–43. Tiffany Stern, 'Was TOTUS MUNDUS AGIT HISTRIONEM Ever the Motto of the Globe Theatre?', *Theatre Notebook*, 51 (1997), 122–7, is more sceptical about whether it was used at the Globe.

CHAPTER 2

1. See Roslyn L. Knutson, 'Falconer to the Little Eyases: A New Date and Commercial Agenda for the "Little Eyases" Passage in *Hamlet*', *Shakespeare Quarterly*, 46 (1995), 1–31.

2. For an overview of the practices of the professional companies on their travels, see Gurr, *The Shakespearian Playing Companies*, ch. 3.

3. For a full account of the history and functions of the Revels Office, see Richard Dutton, *Mastering the Revels: The Regulation and Censorship of English Renaissance Drama* (Basingstoke, 1991).

4. Harold Jenkins (ed.), *Hamlet* (London, 1982), 345–6; Philip Edwards (ed.), *Hamlet* (Cambridge, 1984), 190–2; G. R. Hibbard, (ed.), *Hamlet* (Oxford, 1987), Appendix A, 362–5.

5. For a survey of the evidence for the expected length of early performances, see Gurr, *The Shakespearian Playing Companies*, 81–3.

6. *The Control and Censorship of Caroline Drama*, ed. N. W. Bawcutt (Oxford, 1996).

7. See e.g. E. K. Chambers, *The Elizabethan Stage*, 4 vols. (Oxford, 1923), iv. 208, 219, 225, 295.

8. This term was used in 1617 of the enclosed Blackfriars theatre. The 'middle region' where army captains might seat themselves (Henry Fitzgeoffery, *Satyres, and Satyricall Epigrams*, 1617, E8v), if it was the middle of the three levels of galleries, was where Henslowe located the 'gentlemen's rooms' at

the Fortune, which ranked next to the 'lords' rooms' on the stage balcony.

9. See John Orrell, 'Nutshells at the Rose', *Theatre Research International*, 17 (1992), 8–14.

10. See Andrew Gurr, '*The Tempest*'s Tempest at Blackfriars', *Shakespeare Survey*, 41 (1988), 91–102.

11. See *Henslowe's Diary*, 278.

12. Mark Eccles, 'Elizabethan Actors iv: S to End', *Notes and Queries*, 238 (1993), 171.

13. This copy is examined by Leslie Thomson, 'A Quarto "Marked for Performance": Evidence of What?', *Medieval and Renaissance Drama in English*, 8 (1996), 176–210.

14. *The First Folio of Shakespeare: The Norton Facsimile*, 2nd edn, 1996, p. xxx.

15. *Alphonsus King of Aragon*, 1599 (Malone Society Reprints, 1926), 2109–10.

16. See Andrew Gurr, 'The Date and the Expected Venue of *Romeo and Juliet*', *Shakespeare Survey*, 49 (1996), 15–25.

17. See Ch. 5b, 'Masques, Shows and Ghost Scenes'.

CHAPTER 3

1. *Ben Jonson*, ed. C. H. Herford and P. and E. Simpson, 11 vols. (Oxford, 1925–52), viii. 403.

2. The full lists can be found in *Henslowe's Diary*, 291–94, 317–23, and 325.

3. David Bradley, *From text to performance in the Elizabethan theatre. Preparing the play for the stage* (Cambridge, 1992), 37, 178–80.

4. For a discussion of this distinction in relation to stage directions, see Alan C. Dessen, *Recovering Shakespeare's Theatrical Vocabulary*, (Cambridge, 1995), 55–9.

5. For an extended discussion of the uses of the sick chair, see Alan C. Dessen, *Recovering Shakespeare's Theatrical Vocabulary*, ch. 6.

6. See Ch. 5b, 'Hiding Behind the Hangings'.

7. See *Henslowe's Diary*, 319, 312, and Andrew Gurr, *The Shakespearean Stage 1574–1642*, 183.

8. *Shakespeare's Plutarch*, ed. T. J. B. Spencer (Harmondsworth, 1964), 279–80. It is quoted in the original spelling in G. Bullough, *Narrative and Dramatic Sources of Shakespeare*, 8 vols. (London, 1957–75), viii. 309–10.

9. *Henslowe's Diary*, 101.

10. *The Diary of John Manningham of the Middle Temple: 1602–1603*, ed. Robert P. Sorlien (Hanover, NH, 1976), 187.

11. *Knavery in All Trades* (1664), iii. i.

12. *Henslowe's Diary*, 319.

13. Charles Edelman, *Brawl Ridiculous: Swordfighting in Shakespeare's Plays*

(Manchester, 1992), 158–60, 169–71.

14. *Henslowe's Diary*, 319–20.
15. Ibid. 217.
16. Ibid. 323.

CHAPTER 4

1. Philip Edwards (ed.), *Hamlet*, 140 n.
2. Stanley Wells and Gary Taylor, *William Shakespeare: A Textual Companion* (Oxford, 1987), 406.
3. Q1 does not provide an exit stage direction for them. For some possible forms of their exit in the Q1 version, see Ch. 6a.
4. *The Merchant* Q1 contains a duplicated entry stage direction (E2v), and the second entry can be thought of as an abandoned first thought. See M. M. Mahood (ed.), *The Merchant of Venice* (Cambridge, 1987), 110n.
5. See Stanley Wells, 'Editorial Treatment of Foul-paper Texts: *Much Ado about Nothing* as Test Case', *Review of English Studies*, 31 (1980), 1–16.
6. See Paul Nelsen, 'Positing Pillars at the Globe', *Shakespeare Quarterly*, 48 (1997), 324–35.
7. Michael Drayton, Richard Hathaway, Anthony Munday, and Robert Wilson, *1 Sir John Oldcastle*, ed. Percy Simpson (Malone Society Reprints, 1908).
8. See John Orrell, 'The Theaters', in *A New History of Early English Drama*, ed. John D. Cox and David Scott Kastan (New York, 1997), 93–112, esp. 105.
9. For a detailed discussion of the main acting area, see Ch. 1c.
10. See Alan Brissenden (ed.), *As You Like It* (Oxford, 1993), 116 n.
11. We need some economical and exact terms to describe those characters making entrances and those making exits. We use 'enterers' and 'exiters' as the most economical denotations. Warren D. Smith uses 'enterer' and 'exiter' regularly in *Shakespeare's Playhouse Practice* (Hanover, NH, 1975).
12. Those instances in which a character exits to investigate a noise made within, and those in which a character exits to obtain expected information are also classified under this type.
13. Alan C. Dessen's discussion of the possibility that Seyton does not leave the stage is interesting. See *Elizabethan Stage Conventions and Modern Interpreters* (Cambridge, 1984), 5–7; *Recovering Shakespeare's Theatrical Vocabulary*, 93–4.
14. See W. W. Greg, *Dramatic Documents from the Elizabethan Playhouses* (Oxford, 1931), i. 216–17. However, we must take seriously William B. Long's warning about the danger of making generalizations about what playhouse book-keepers would or would not do. See e.g. '*John a Kent and*

John a Cumber: An Elizabethan Playbook and Its Implications', in *Shakespeare and Dramatic Tradition*, ed. W. R. Elton and William B. Long (Newark, 1989), 125–43.

15. Fredson Bowers, 'Authority, Copy, and Transmission in Shakespeare's Texts', in *Shakespeare Study Today*, ed. Georgianna Ziegler (New York, 1986), 7–36, esp. 19–20.

16. The examples in which the number of lines is between nought and two are as follows. The abbreviations of titles of plays are those used in C. T. Onions, *A Shakespeare Glossary*, enlarged and revised throughout by Robert D. Eagleson (Oxford, 1986). 'm' added to a line number designates a part-line. Those marked ? are doubtful examples.

A^+ = 0: *TGV* 4.4.115–115 (attendant)?; *1 H4* 2.5.486[328]–486 (Bardolph)
A^+ = 1: *2H4* 2.4.371[369]–372 (Bardolph); *HAM* 5.2.301m[264]–301 (Osric); *LR* 1.4.46–7 (knight)
A^+ = 2: *SHR* Ind. 1.72–4 (servingman); *SHR* 5.2.83–5 (Biondello)
B = 0: *SHR* 5.1.84–84 (servant–officer)?; *2H6* 5.1.145–145 (attendant–Salisbury, Warwick); *R2* 4.1.1m–1m (lord–Bagot)?; *1H4* 2.5.511–511 (Hostess–Sheriff); *TRO* 4.2.60–60 (Pandarus–Troilus)?; *TIM* 1.2.118–118 (servant–Cupid)?; *PER* 21.8–8 (gentlemen–Lysimachus)?; *WT* 4.4.340–340 (servant–satyrs)?; *H8* 4.2.109m–109m (Griffith–Caputius)?
B = 1: *AYL* 1.1.89–90 (Dennis–Charles); *OTH* 3.1.38[38m]–39 (Iago–Emilia); *AWW* 2.1.90–1 (Lafew–Helen)?; *ANT* 4.2.9m–10m (one–servitors)?; *H8* 2.2.116[117]–117 (Wolsey–Gardiner)
B = 2: *SHR* 5.2.101–3 (Grumio–Katherine); *JN* 1.1.47–9m (Sheriff–Falconbridge, Bastard); *HAM* 4.6.3–5 (attendant–sailor); *TN* 1.5.158–60 (Malvolio–Viola); *TN* 3.4.14m–15[14m] (Maria–Malvolio)?; *TRO* 4.7.41m–42 (Aeneas–Troilus)?; *MM* 4.2.58[57]–60 (Pompey–Claudio); *AWW* 5.3.154–6m[154] (attendant–Bertram); *TIM* 1.2.125–7 (Cupid–masque); *PER* 4.80–2 (lord–Pericles); *WT* 2.2.2m–4m (gentleman–jailer); *WT* 2.2.21–3m (jailer–Emilia); *H8* 5.1.83–5 (Denny–Cranmer).

17. A = 3: *2H6* 4.1.140–3 (Whitmore); *R3* 1.4.265–8 (1. Murderer); *R3* 3.7.91–4 (Catesby)?; *2H4* 2.4.385–8 (Bardolph)
A = 4: *TIT* 5.2.160–4 (Titus); *WIV* 1.4.33–7 (Rugby)?; *WIV* 4.2.93[91]–7 (Mrs Ford); *2H4* 2.4.207–12 (Bardolph); *OTH* 1.2.49m–53m (Othello); *LR* 1.4.269–73 (Lear); *COR* 4.5.2–6 (1. servingman); *TMP* 1.1.32–6[35m] (Sebastian, Antonio, Gonzalo).

18. Because *All's Well*, 2.1 is a ceremonial scene, it is likely that the King sits on the chair of state. Lafew would stand beside or behind the royal chair.

19. For a similar comment, see Joan Ozark Holmer ' "Draw, if you be men": Saviolo's Significance for *Romeo and Juliet*', *Shakespeare Quarterly*, 45 (1994), 163–89, esp. 180.

20. There is the speculative possibility that the roles of Chorus and Friar were actually doubled in the original performance. For the Q2 version, T. J. King assigns these two roles to the same actor. See *Casting Shakespeare's Plays*, 174.

21. Dessen, *Recovering Shakespeare's Theatrical Vocabulary*, 65–6.

22. See ibid. 48–9.

23. In the F1 version, however, the captain and the rest of the army probably use the same door for their exits. For one thing, the split exit at the end of the scene would have been undesirable for the smoothness of the scene change. For another, a short march scene ordinarily consists of a general entrance by one door and a general exit by the other door. See also Ch. 7e.

24. See Ch. 2i.

25. For the possibility that the King and Polonius did not really exit but went behind the arras, see Ch. 5b, 'Hiding behind the Hangings'.

26. See *Shakespeare at the Globe: 1599–1609* (New York, 1962), 176–8.

27. See ibid. 179.

28. See Thomas Heywood, *The Captives*, ed. Arthur Brown (Malone Society Reprints, 1953).

29. John Marston, *1 & 2 Antonio and Mellida*, ed. W. W. Greg (Malone Society Reprints, 1921).

30. See Gary Taylor and John Jowett, *Shakespeare Reshaped: 1616–1623* (Oxford, 1993), 151–71, 239–41.

31. e.g. *Julius Caesar* F1 has a stage direction reading '*Enter Caesar, Antony for the Course, Calphurnia, Portia, Decius, Cicero, Brutus, Cassius, Caska, a Soothsayer: after them Murellus and Flavius*' (1.2.0).

32. The examples of 'None' in which the number of lines is between nought and six are as follows. Those marked ? are doubtful instances in which it is not certain whether the exit and entrance actually occur or not, or whether there really is a scene-break between the exit and the entrance.

    None = 0: *SHR* 3.2.127–3.3.0 (Lucentio)?; *TIT* 3.2.84–4.1.0 (Young Lucius, Lavinia); *R3* 3.3.24–3.4.0 (Ratcliffe); *CYM* 5.5.94–5.5.94 (Posthumus, jailers)?; *TMP* 4.1.264–5.1.0 (Prospero, Ariel)

    None = 3: *TIM* 3.4.96–3.5.0 (Timon)

    None = 4: *SHR* 4.4.67[66]–4.5.0 (Biondello)?; *CYM* 2.4.149m–2.5.0 (Posthumus)

    None = 5: *1H4* 2.2.89–2.3.5 (Falstaff, etc.)?; *HAM* 1.4.63–1.5.0 (Ghost, Hamlet)?; *TRO* 5.1.95–5.2.5[8] (Thersites)

    None = 6: *SHR* 3.1.84–3.2.0 (Bianca); *H5* 1.1.99–1.2.6 (Archbishop, Ely); *HAM* 5.1.291–5.2.0 (Horatio); *TRO* 5.5.43–5.6.0 (Ajax); *TRO* 5.5.44–5.6.1 (Diomedes); *MM* 3.1.538–4.1.6 (Duke); *ANT* 4.15.138–4.16.6m (Diomedes)

33. See Wilfred T. Jewkes, *Act Division in Elizabethan and Jacobean Plays: 1583–1616* (New York, 1958); Taylor and Jowett, *Shakespeare Reshaped*, 3–50; and Andrew Gurr, '*The Tempest*'s Tempest at Blackfriars', 91–102.

34. In *Pericles*, the actor playing Pericles must take off the wig and false beard he has worn between his exit at the end of scene 21 and his re-entrance at line 16 of scene 22. Since this costume change is very simple, sixteen lines would provide enough time.

35. For a similar conclusion, see Irwin Smith, 'Their Exits and Reentrances', *Shakespeare Quarterly*, 18 (1967), 7–16.

CHAPTER 5

1. Bernard Beckerman, 'Theatrical Plots and Elizabethan Stage Practice', in *Shakespeare and Dramatic Tradition* (Newark, 1989), 109–24. See also W. B. Long, '*John a Kent and John a Cumber*', ibid. 136–7.

2. Barnabe Barnes, *The Devil's Charter* (Tudor Facsimile Texts, 1913).

3. John Orrell, 'The Polarity of the Globe's Stage' (a paper read at the first ISGC conference, 1995).

4. See Alan C. Dessen, *Recovering Shakespeare's Theatrical Vocabulary*, 48–9.

5. George Chapman, *The Revenge of Bussy D'Ambois* (Scolar Press Facsimiles, 1968).

6. *1 The Troublesome Reign of King John* (Tudor Facsimile Texts, 1911).

7. Thomas Dekker, *The Dramatic Works*, ed. Fredson Bowers, 4 vols. (Cambridge, 1953), i.

8. Thomas Heywood, *The Dramatic Works*, 4 vols. (London, 1874; repr., New York, 1964), iv.

9. Thomas Heywood, *The Dramatic Works*, ii.

10. See e.g. *The Merchant of Venice*, 2.2.168; *Hamlet*, 2.2.221–2.

11. See e.g. *The Two Gentlemen of Verona*, 3.1.0–2; *Romeo and Juliet*, 2.4.17–20; *1 Henry IV*, 3.2.0–3; *Hamlet*, 4.5.109–14.

12. For similar examples, see *2 Henry IV*, 2.4.385–8 and *King Lear*, 4.5.278–84.

13. See e.g. *The Two Gentlemen of Verona*, 1.3.87–91; 2.2.18–20; *Romeo and Juliet*, 1.3.101–7; *Much Ado about Nothing*, 3.5.50–3; *Cymbeline*, 1.3.38–41.

14. T. S. Dorsch (ed.), *The Comedy of Errors* (Cambridge, 1988), 24.

15. It is possible that the Apothecary's shop was represented by the central opening rather than a flanking door. For a detailed discussion of shop scenes, see Dessen, *Recovering Shakespeare's Theatrical Vocabulary*, 155–9.

16. See Julie Hankey (ed.), *Richard III: Plays in Performance* (London, 1981), 200.

17. For the 'S' rule and the 'L' rule, see Ch. 7a.

18. Although *Timon*, 5.4 is an outdoor scene, the use of the curtains seems possible. See E. K. Chambers, *The Elizabethan Stage*, iii. 133.

19. Stanley Wells (ed.), *A Midsummer Night's Dream* (Harmondsworth, 1967), 138. An alternative possibility is broached by R. A. Foakes, who thinks that if Titania remained in full view of the audience, but unnoticed by the lovers or mechanicals, this indeed would fit in with the play's concern with illusion and theatricality. See Foakes (ed.), *A Midsummer Night's Dream* (Cambridge, 1984), 73 n.

20. Francis Beaumont and John Fletcher, *The Dramatic Works*, gen. ed. Fredson Bowers (Cambridge, 1966), i.

21. For a similar conclusion, see Bernard Beckerman, *Shakespeare at the Globe, 1599–1609*, 193–5. See also Hibbard (ed.), *Hamlet*, 239 n.

22. Since in this scene excursions occur between a split exit and a split entrance, the excursions must have been made as a confrontation, not as a pursuit.

23. Thomas Dekker, *The Dramatic Works*.

24. See David Bradley, *From Text to Performance in the Elizabethan Theatre*, 171.

25. For the plot and the Quarto text, see *The Battle of Alcazar*, ed. W. W. Greg (Malone Society Reprints, 1907) and *Two Elizabethan Abridgements: The Battle of Alcazar & Orlando Furioso*, ed. W. W. Greg (Malone Society Reprints, 1922).

26. When we consider this question, what part of the auditorium provided the best seats is a very important factor. For a discussion of the view from the lords' room, see Ch. 1b. Gabriel Egan, however, argues that the likeliest location is the extreme end of the lowest auditorium gallery nearest the stage. See 'The Situation of the "Lords Room": A Revaluation', *Review of English Studies*, 48 (1997), 297–309.

27. See John H. Astington, 'Descent Machinery in the Playhouses', *Medieval & Renaissance Drama in England*, 2 (1985), 119–33. See also Ch. 3b.

28. Marston, *1 & 2 Antonio and Mellida*, ed. Greg (Malone Society Reprints, 1921).

29. For the two ways of staging a bed, see Richard Hosley, 'The Staging of Desdemona's Bed', *Shakespeare Quarterly*, 14 (1963), 57–65; Andrew Gurr, *The Shakespearean Stage 1574–1642*, 188.

30. See Ch. 2i.

31. e.g. in scenes 18 and 22 of *Pericles*, if the curtained space represents the monument of Marina and the temple of Diana, Gower might not use it for his entrances and exits in these scenes. In the finale of *Henry V*, if the central opening is used for the general exit, the Chorus would enter from a flanking door in order to speak the Epilogue.

32. See J. H. P. Pafford (ed.), *The Winter's Tale* (London, 1963), 168.
33. See Ch. 7d.
34. See Ch. 7f.
35. See Stephen Orgel (ed.), *The Tempest* (Oxford, 1987), 118 n.
36. The only alternative is that, since the king and three lords have offered to escort the queen and three ladies on their way home (5.2.860), these four pairs of lovers might exit together through the central opening, while the characters of spring and winter exit separately through the side doors. The Braggart's speech 'You that way; we this way' (5.2.915), which seems to indicate exits by the flanking doors, is missing from Q1.
37. In the finale of *Pericles*, a prop altar was probably placed in the central opening, and in the finale of *The Winter's Tale*, the curtained space was used to reveal Hermione's statue. In the case of *The Winter's Tale*, however, since Hermione comes forth from the discovery space, it is not entirely impossible that the central opening was used for the general exit, though whether the statue's plinth from which she had descended was removed to clear the exit space is a question. What is certain is that there were blue-coated stage hands who 'invisibly' removed such properties. For the 'invisible' stage hands, see Gurr, *The Shakespearean Stage*, 189.

CHAPTER 6

1. Gloucester has to change costumes for the next scene. Gary Taylor argues that an interval between the acts makes F1's omission of the dialogue of the servants possible. See Taylor and Jowett, *Shakespeare Reshaped*, 48–9.
2. We are indebted to Raymond Powell for these interpretations.
3. See Gary Taylor, '*King Lear*: The Date and Authorship of the Folio Version', in Taylor and Michael Warren (eds.), *The Division of the Kingdoms: Shakespeare's Two Versions of 'King Lear'* (Oxford, 1983), 424; René Weis (ed.), *King Lear: A Parallel Text Edition* (London, 1993), 24–5.
4. See Wells and Taylor, *Textual Companion*, 281, 284.
5. See Wells (ed.), *A Midsummer Night's Dream*, 141.
6. See George Walton Williams, 'Preface—by Way of a Prefix', in Williams (ed.), *Shakespeare's Speech Headings: Speaking the Speech in Shakespeare's Plays* (Newark, 1997), pp. xi–xxiv, esp. p. xx.
7. There are some opening stage directions that include the names of characters who should arrive a few lines later: e.g. '*Enter King of* Fairies, *and* Robin goodfellow' (*A Midsummer Night's Dream* Q1, 3.2.0), '*Enter Hamlet, Rosencraus, and others*' (*Hamlet* Q2, 4.2.0).
8. See Sir Arthur Quiller-Couch and John Dover Wilson (eds.), *All's Well*

That Ends Well (Cambridge, 1929), 17, 130; Susan Synder (ed.), *All's Well That Ends Well* (Oxford, 1994), 100 n. Unlike these editors, we do not think that the nine-line speech should be spoken as an aside.

9. John C. Adams, 'The Staging of *The Tempest*, III. iii', *Review of English Studies*, 14 (1938), 404–19, esp. 414–5.
10. Orgel (ed.), *The Tempest*, 164 n. See also Irwin Smith, *Shakespeare's Blackfriars Playhouse* (London, 1964), 412.
11. Michael Hattaway (ed.), *1 Henry VI* (Cambridge, 1990), 128 n.
12. Adams, 'The Staging of *The Tempest*, III. iii', 416–9. See also Peter Holland, 'The Shapeliness of *The Tempest*', *Essays in Criticism*, 45 (1995), 208–29, esp. 214–5.

CHAPTER 7

1. See *Shakespeare at the Globe, 1599–1609*, 72–3.
2. See Tim Fitzpatrick, 'Shakespeare's Exploitation of a Two-Door Stage: *Macbeth*', *Theatre Research International*, 20 (1995), 207–30.
3. For a full discussion of this question, see Ch. 5a.
4. See for instance the booth stage and its audience in 'Kermesse' by David Vinckboons, *c.*1601–11, in the Herzog Anton Ulrich Museum at Braunschweig; or Pieter Breughel the Elder's 'Feast of St George' (*c.*1560), with its curtained booth stage.
5. Thomas Nashe, *Pierce Penilesse*, 1592, 'A Tale of a wise Justice', in *Works*, ed. R. B. McKerrow, 5 vols. (London, 1904–10), i. 188; *Praeludium* to Thomas Goffe, *The Careless Shepherdess*, 1656, quoted in G. E. Bentley, *The Jacobean and Caroline Stage*, 7 vols. (Oxford, 1940–68), ii. 541, and iv. 501–5. Goffe died before his play was re-staged. The *Praeludium* was written for the revival at Salisbury Court playhouse in about 1638.
6. For a more detailed study of the uses of the central opening, see Ch. 5b.
7. Thomas Nabbes, in the prologue to his play *Hannibal and Scipio*, written in 1634 for an indoor theatre, assured the women in his audience that his play would not have any of the duels with broadswords and metal shields (targets) then typical of the open-air theatres:

> Nor need you Ladies feare the horrid sight:
> And the more horrid noise of target fight
> By the blue-coated stage-keepers: our spheares
> Have better musick to delight your eares.

The Works of Thomas Nabbes, ed. A. H. Bullen (2 vols., London, 1882–9), i. 190. The stage-hands in their blue coats performed such actions as drawing back the hangings for ceremonial entrances, and made up the numbers for battles on stage.

8. Thomas Dekker in chapter 6 of *The Gull's Hornbook* suggests that entry of the Prologue to announce the start of a play was normally preceded by three trumpet calls. Other references say much the same.

9. The modern assumption that trumpets were chiefly used for battlefield noises is misleading. Most 'alarums' were signalled by drums. Trumpets were ceremonial, to announce heralds (with a 'sennet'), or for royal entrances.

10. i.e. not quite at the medieval *locus*, set back at the *frons*, but nearer the centre, and certainly not with its back to a wall. Thrones in the presence chamber stood well out from the rear wall. As a practical consideration, to have it backed up against the *frons* on stage would of course make it impossible to use the central opening for the royal entry. If this location is correct, its proximity in the stage's centre to the place where the ghost disappeared was a nice irony.

11. There are altogether five references in the play to Denmark being an elective kingdom, the last when the dying Hamlet gives his 'voice' for Fortinbras as the next king. In England inheritance by the law of succession was normal, but this play quietly displaces it from Denmark. That of course has a heavy bearing on the legality of the crown passing to the dead king's brother and not to his son.

12. It has been suggested, rather ingeniously, that these greetings are done in a pretended night scene, with Horatio carrying a flaming torch (because it is 'even'), and that Hamlet's succession of greetings comes as the visitors become visible under Horatio's torch. This underrates the signifying of relative status, which gains in significance when Hamlet insists as they leave that their idea of their 'duty' is really love.

13. Richard Dutton argues that Rosencrantz's claim that the little eyases have displaced 'Hercules and his load too' refers to the insignia. See '*Hamlet, An Apology for Actors*, and The Sign of the Globe', 35–43, and Roslyn L. Knutson, 'Falconer to the Little Eyases', 1–31.

14. *De Republica Anglorum*, ed. Mary Dewar (Cambridge, 1982), 88.

15. See Pauline Kiernan, *Shakespeare's Theory of Drama* (Cambridge, 1996), 116–17.

16. See Ch. 4a.

17. See Ch. 5b.

18. In some passages, such as this one, where the Folio text, which here gives 'your Honestie' while Q1 and Q2 both have 'with honesty', seems inadequate, the Oxford text has been used.

19. For evidence to support their being in this position, see Andrew Gurr,

'Traps and Discoveries at the Globe', *Proceedings of the British Academy*, *94*, 1997, 85–101. An alternative possibility for staging this scene is set out by Michael Shurgot, '"Get you a place": Staging the Mousetrap at the Globe Theatre', *Shakespeare Bulletin*, 12 (Summer 1994), 5–9.

20. See Ch. 2a, and the notes in the New Cambridge *Hamlet*, pp. 16–19, and the one-volume Oxford edition, Appendix A, pp. 362–5.

21. A similar action appears in *Antony and Cleopatra*, 3.8, where the stage direction specifies '*Enter Caesar with his Army, marching*'. Although neither text is specific about who leaves first, it seems most likely that Caesar sends his captain Towrus ahead of him, as Fortinbras does here.

22. See also Ch. 4c.

23. See Ch. 4c. Some interesting speculations about Gertrude's actions after her talk with Hamlet, in particular her withdrawal from Claudius, are in Ellen J. O'Brien, 'Revision by Excision: Rewriting Gertrude', *Shakespeare Survey*, 45 (1993), 27–35.

24. Real herbs would be expected in season, and dried versions where possible in the winter.

25. A mattock for cutting into hard ground and a spade are the instruments specified to open Juliet's tomb for the final scene of *Romeo and Juliet* in the graveyard.

26. See Ch. 4a.

27. An alternative possibility is that the original Osric was played by Will Sly, in 1605 a sharer in the Shakespeare company, and aged at least 30 by the time *Hamlet* was written. In the Induction to Marston's *The Malcontent*, written for its performance at the Globe, Will Sly comes on stage acting an elegant gallant, and asks to speak to the actors, including 'Dick Burbage', the original player of Hamlet. In their exchange he plays Osric's game from 5.2. with his hat, using Osric's own words when he refuses to put it back on his head.

28. For a longer comment on these parallels, see Ch. 2i.

29. For a well-informed analysis of duels, the weapons and procedures, see Charles Edelman, *Brawl Ridiculous*, 181–91.

30. The story of the first Globe burning down in 1613 when a piece of wadding from a 'cannon' caught in the thatch over the galleries is a strong indication that chambers to simulate the noise of cannon firing were positioned at roof level, over the stage.

31. We use the translation by Ernest Schanzer, 'Thomas Platter's Observations on the Elizabethan Stage', *Notes and Queries*, 201 (1956), 465–7.

32. See Andrew Gurr, *The Shakespearian Playing Companies*, 291.

Bibliography and Suggestions for Further Reading

The texts and act, scene and line numbers used for reference to the Shakespeare plays in this book are principally those of the Oxford Shakespeare (*William Shakespeare, The Complete Works*, ed. Stanley Wells and Gary Taylor, Oxford, 1986), the main text of which is also available in the Norton Shakespeare. Quotations from the original texts are from the second *Norton Facsimile: the First Folio of Shakespeare*, ed. Charlton Hinman (New York, 1996), and for the quartos from *Shakespeare's Plays in Quarto: A Facsimile Edition of Copies Mainly from the Henry E. Huntington Library*, ed. Michael J. B. Allen and Kenneth Muir (Berkeley and Los Angeles, 1981). The texts of other plays are usually taken from the Malone Society Reprints editions, as listed in the notes.

For other materials, the chief sources of information are G. E. Bentley, *The Jacobean and Caroline Stage* (7 vols., Oxford, 1940–68), E. K. Chambers, *The Elizabethan Stage* (4 vols., Oxford, 1923), *Henslowe's Diary*, ed. R. A. Foakes and R. T. Rickert (Cambridge, 1961), and *Dramatic Documents from the Elizabethan Playhouses*, ed. W. W. Greg (Oxford, 1930). All the surviving pictures of the theatres and staging are reproduced with commentary in R. A. Foakes, *Illustrations of the English Stage 1580–1642* (London, 1985).

General studies of the early conditions for Shakespearian playing include Andrew Gurr, *The Shakespearean Stage 1574–1642* (3rd edn., Cambridge, 1992); *A New History of Early English Drama*, ed. John D. Cox and David Scott Kastan (New York, 1997); and Robert Weimann, *Shakespeare and the Popular Tradition in the Theater*, ed. and trans. Robert D. Schwartz (London, 1978). Studies of the early playhouses can be found in John Orrell, *The Human Stage: English Theatre Design, 1567–1640* (Cambridge, 1988); and *The Theatres of Inigo Jones and John Webb* (Cambridge, 1985). More particular studies include David Bradley, *From Text to Performance in the Elizabethan Theatre* (Cambridge, 1992); Richard Dutton, *Mastering the Revels: The Regulation and Censorship of English Renaissance Drama* (Basingstoke, 1991); Charles Edelman, *Brawl Ridiculous: Swordfighting in Shakespeare's Plays* (Manchester, 1992); Andrew Gurr, *Playgoing in Shakespeare's London* (Cambridge, 2nd edn., 1996), and *The Shakespearian Playing Companies* (Oxford, 1996); Pauline Kiernan, *Shakespeare's Theory of Drama* (Cambridge, 1996); and T. J. King, *Casting*

Shakespeare's Plays: London Actors and their Roles, 1590–1632 (Cambridge, 1992). Scholarly works with value for the study of early staging include Bernard Beckerman, *Shakespeare at the Globe, 1599–1609* (New York, 1963); Alan C. Dessen, *Elizabethan Stage Conventions and Modern Interpreters* (Cambridge, 1984) and *Recovering Shakespeare's Theatrical Vocabulary* (Cambridge, 1995); and Warren D. Smith, *Shakespeare's Playhouse Practice* (Hanover, NH. 1975).